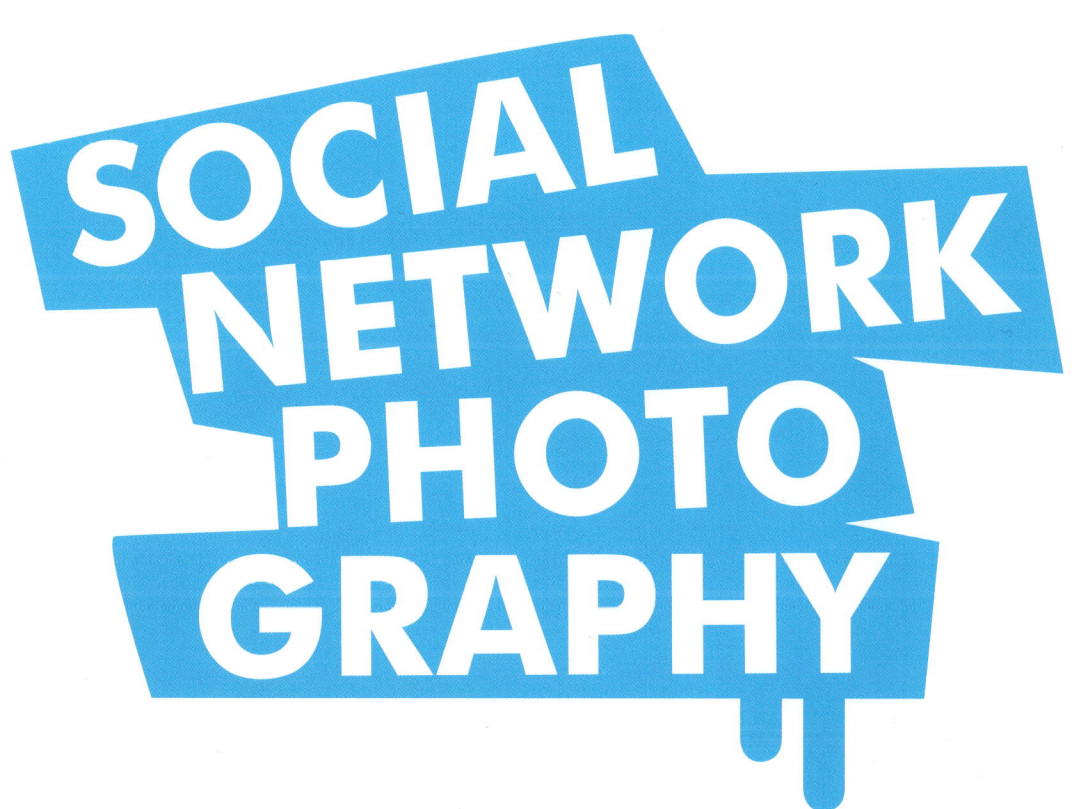

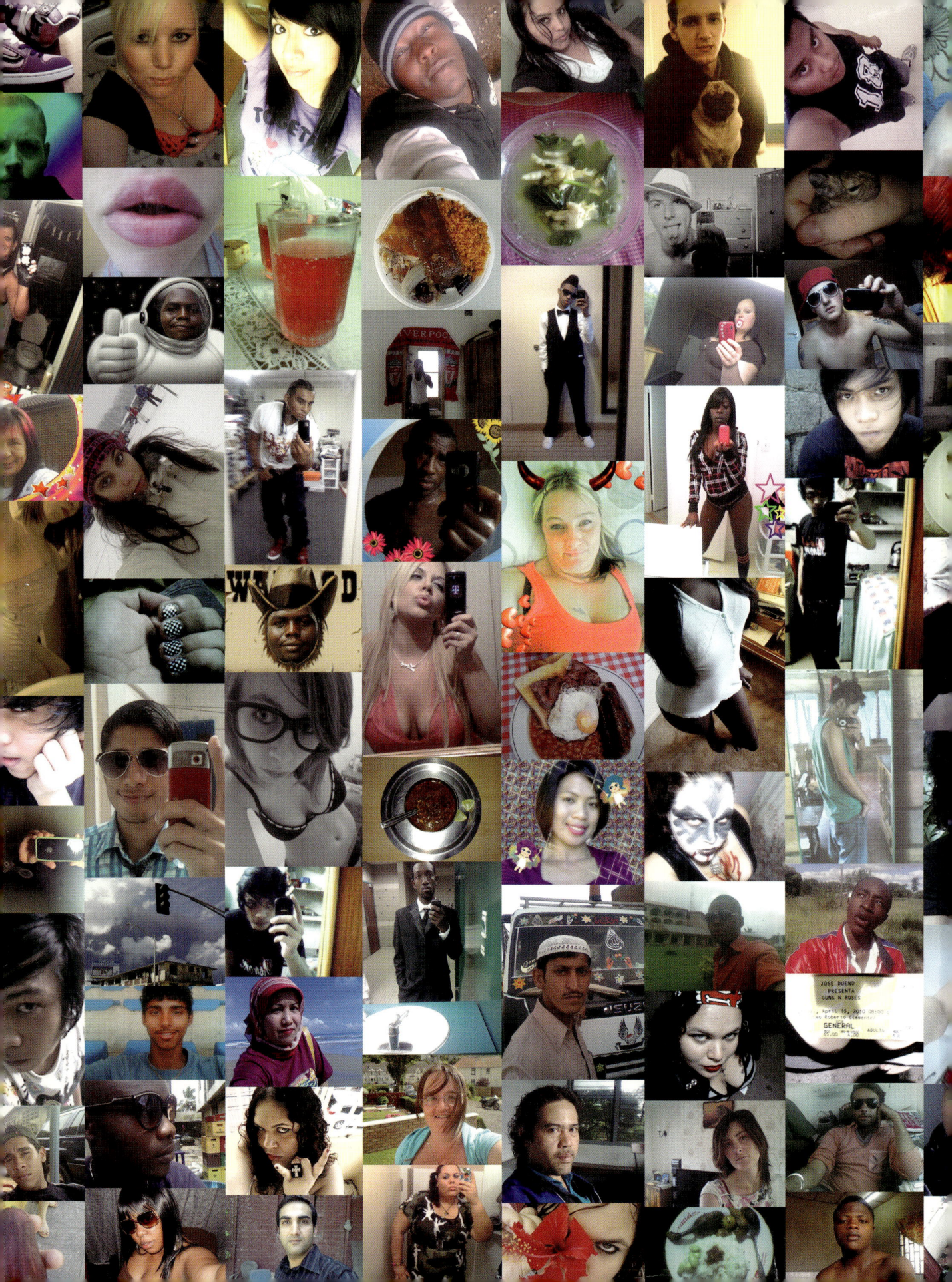

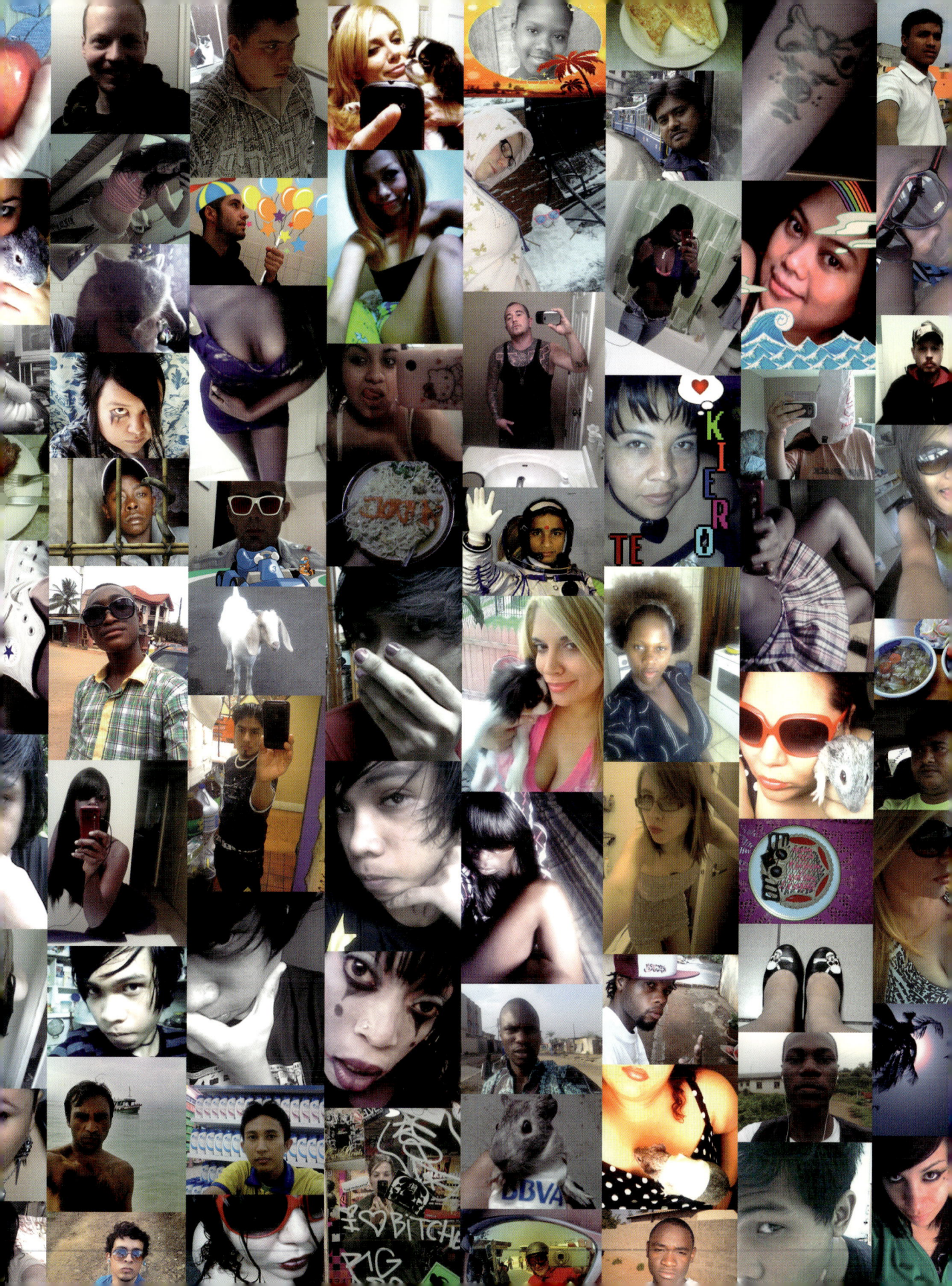

Wir danken unseren Freunden in aller Welt, dass sie uns das Recht zum Publizieren ihrer Bilder erteilten.

Um die Authentizität der Bilder zu bewahren, wurden diese im Buch im Original verwendet, d. h. genauso, wie sie online veröffentlicht wurden.

Many thanks to all our friends worldwide for granting us the rights to publish their photos.

In order to retain the authenticity of the photos,
they are shown in the book in their original form, i.e.
exactly as they were published online.

INTRO
FOREWORD | HISTORY
VORWORT | GESCHICHTE
9

ARM'S LENGTH
ONE HANDED | TWO HANDED | ARM IN SUNGLASSES
EINHÄNDIG | ZWEIHÄNDIG | ARM IN SONNENBRILLE
17

ME IN THE MIRROR
FACE COVERED | CAMERA CHECK | MIRROR SHAPES | PROS
GESICHT VERDECKT | KAMERA-CHECK | SPIEGELFORMEN | PROFIS
47

LOCATION
SURROUNDINGS | MY ROOM | MY PROFESSION | ON THE ROAD
UMGEBUNG | MEIN ZIMMER | MEIN BERUF | UNTERWEGS
87

MESSAGES
LOVE | AUTHENTICITY | HAND GESTURES
LIEBE | AUTHENTIZITÄT | HANDZEICHEN
125

STYLEZ
MY STYLE | MY TATTOO
MEIN STYLE | MEIN TATTOO
145

STUFF
MY STUFF | MY MEAL | ME & MY PET
MEIN ZEUG | MEIN ESSEN | ICH & MEIN HAUSTIER
167

PICTURE ENHANCEMENTS
187

PEOPLE
193

OUTRO
FACTS | ABOUT THE EDITORS | ACKNOWLEDGEMENTS | IMPRINT
FAKTEN | ÜBER DIE AUTOREN | DANKSAGUNG | IMPRESSUM
274

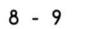

HEUTE SCHON BILDER HOCHGELADEN?
UPLOADED ANY PICTURES TODAY?

BY SABINE IRRGANG

Die Möglichkeit, mit dem Handy Fotos zu machen und diese mit wenigen Klicks in einem sozialen Netzwerk zu veröffentlichen, hat sich zu einem neuen Gesellschaftsphänomen entwickelt.

Besonders Selbstporträts, die in sozialen Netzwerken weltweit als Profilbilder hochgeladen werden, sind täglich neue Belege dieser Entwicklung.

Da fast jeder Nutzer eines sozialen Netzwerks auch ein Handy besitzt, werden Selbstporträts von sehr vielen Menschen publiziert. Andere Mitglieder der Netzwerke wiederum betrachten, bewerten und kommentieren diese Bilder. So entsteht eine völlig neue Art der Kommunikation.

Wir haben in diesem Buch die schönsten, coolsten, überraschendsten und eindrucksvollsten Bilder aus verschiedenen sozialen Netzwerken zusammengestellt.

So entstehen Einblicke und Eindrücke, wie sich Menschen aus der ganzen Welt in sozialen Netzwerken darstellen – sei es für Freunde, für die Familie, für Geschäftspartner oder auch für ein unbekanntes öffentliches Publikum.

Unsere Anwendungsempfehlung:
überraschen lassen – inspirieren lassen – kreativ sein.

Being able to take photos on a mobile phone, which can then be published onto a social network in just a couple of clicks, has led to a new social phenomenon.

Evidence of this development is seen again and again, on a daily basis, particularly taking the form of self-portraits which are uploaded as social network profile pictures all around the globe.

As the vast majority of social network members also own a mobile phone, self-portraits are made public by a huge number of people. These pictures are then viewed, rated and commented on by other network members, which, in turn, is giving rise to a completely new form of communication.

In this book we have combined the coolest, most beautiful, surprising and striking images from a variety of social networks.

These images provide insights and impressions of how people all around the world present themselves in social networks - whether for friends, family, colleagues or an unknown public.

Our recommendations for use:
be surprised – be inspired – get creative.

SOCIAL NETWORK PHOTOGRAPHY

Mit Beginn des 21. Jahrhunderts hat sich weltweit ein Phänomen entwickelt, das weder geplant noch absehbar war.

Aus zwei fundamentalen Änderungen unseres gesellschaftlichen Verhaltens – der sich schnell verbreitenden weltweiten Nutzung von sozialen Netzwerken und dem Verkauf von Milliarden von Handys und Smartphones mit integrierter Kamera und Internetzugang – entstand innerhalb von nur wenigen Jahren eine neue Art der Kommunikation, die das Teilen von Bildern, Eindrücken und Gedanken mit Familie, Freunden oder auch der ganzen Welt in den Vordergrund rückte.

Als Maßstab für die Qualität dieser Mitteilungen dienen Likes, Votes, Tweets, Retweets und Kommentare anderer User.

Diese neue Form des gesellschaftlichen Miteinanders ist aus dem modernen Alltag nicht mehr wegzudenken, macht viele Nutzer nahezu süchtig und hat wirtschaftliche wie politische Auswirkungen.

Unser Buch widmet sich der Social Network Photography und hier speziell dem Selbstporträt als eine neue Form der Fotografie, die den Zeitgeist per Bild transportiert.

The start of the 21st century saw the development of a worldwide phenomenon which was neither planned nor foreseeable.

Within only a couple of years, the fusion of two fundamental changes in our social behaviour – the quickly spreading international use of social networks and the sale of billions of mobile phones and smartphones featuring integrated cameras and internet access – has created a new form of communication, which has promoted the sharing of pictures, impressions and thoughts with family, friends or even the entire world.

This shared information is assessed through other users' likes, votes, tweets, re-tweets and comments.

Nowadays it would be hard to imagine life without this new kind of social community. For many users, social networks prove to be addictive. Furthermore, they have economic and political consequences.

Our book is dedicated to Social Network Photography, in particular to self-portraits as a new form of photography which uses pictures to convey the spirit of the times.

Sabine Irrgang beschäftigt sich als Geschäftsführerin eines internationalen Social-Media-Unternehmens mit den rechtlichen und technischen Aspekten der Veröffentlichung von Bildern in Social Networks.

Die Fotografin Laura Piantoni ist durch ihre Arbeit als Bildredakteurin bei einem sozialen Netzwerk auf das weltweite Phänomen der Social Network Photography aufmerksam geworden und beschäftigt sich seitdem mit dem Thema „Social Art".

Sabine Irrgang [I] und Laura Piantoni [P] im Gespräch:

[P] *Mit der wachsenden Popularität sozialer Netzwerke wie Facebook oder Twitter und deren Möglichkeiten, persönliche Profile anzulegen und Bilder hochzuladen, entstand die Notwendigkeit eines Profilfotos. Eine Art Visitenkarte oder auch selbst gewähltes Spiegelbild, aufgrund dessen einen andere Nutzer beurteilen und definieren. Wo vorher ein Selbstauslöser in der Kamera benutzt wurde oder ein Mensch den anderen fotografiert hat, ist heute ein neuer Fokus: das Selbstporträt mit dem Handy. Nebenbei durch Ausprobieren und Nachmachen entstanden, verbreiteten sich Fotos mit einer eigenen Bildsprache als Profilbilder – und zwar das Armlängen-Selbstporträt und das Selbstporträt über einen Spiegel. Wie fing das denn bei itsmy an?*

[I] Wir haben im Jahr 2004 einen ersten Service gelauncht, bei dem Nutzer ihre Handyfotos hochladen konnten, um sie mit verschiedenen Bilderrahmen zu verzieren. Damals gab es diese Möglichkeit noch nicht auf dem Handy, deshalb haben wir ein solches Angebot zur Verfügung gestellt. Die ersten Fotos waren meist Hund, Katze, Kind oder das Frühstück und schließlich fotografierte man sich selbst. Im ersten Schritt konnten andere Nutzer für die Bilder voten, im nächsten dann auch Kommentare dazu abgeben. Sehr schnell gab es

As Managing Director of an international social media company, Sabine Irrgang deals with the legal and technical aspects of publishing images on social networks.

Photographer Laura Piantoni became aware of the global phenomenon of Social Network Photography through her role as picture editor for a social network. Since then she has devoted herself to the topic of social art.

Sabine Irrgang [I] and Laura Piantoni [P] talk about their project:

[P] *The growing popularity of social networks such as Facebook or Twitter and the opportunities they offer to create personal profiles and upload photos bring about the need for a profile picture. This is a type of business card or self-chosen mirror image, on the basis of which the user is judged and defined by others. Modern technology means you no longer have to set camera timers or rely on someone else to take a picture of you: today, all you need for your self-portrait is a mobile phone. Photos demonstrating their own visual language incidentally came to emerge as profile pictures through trial and error and imitation - self-portraits taken at arm's length, and the mirror image self-portrait. So how did this all start at itsmy?*

[I] We first launched a service in 2004 where users could upload photos from their mobile phones and enhance them using a selection of photo frames. At that time, mobile phones didn't offer this feature, which is why we decided to offer it. The first photos tended to be of dogs, cats, children or breakfast; later people began to take pictures of themselves. At first, other users could vote for pictures; later, they were able to leave comments. It wasn't long before some users began publishing pornography, drug abuse, scenes of violence, or other similar imagery. This is still something which is spontaneously reacted to today through other users reporting abuse. The option to report

Nutzer, die auch Pornografie, Drogenmissbrauch, Gewaltszenen und Ähnliches veröffentlichten. Die anderen Nutzer reagieren darauf auch heute noch spontan und melden Missbrauch. Diese Möglichkeit zum Missbrauchmelden musste man gleichzeitig mit der Möglichkeit schaffen, die Bilder zu veröffentlichen, um unter anderem minderjährige Nutzer zu schützen, aber auch zum Schutz von Eigentums- und Persönlichkeitsrechten. Es sind die heute allseits bekannten „Nutzer melden"-, „Bild melden"-Links in sozialen Netzwerken. Bearbeitet werden die Meldungen von speziell trainierten Bildredaktionen. Auch bei uns wurde eine Bildredaktion geschaffen.

[P] *Vor einigen Jahren waren es noch relativ wenige Fotos, da nur ein paar Leute eine Handykamera hatten und die öffentliche Kommunikation mit Bildern noch nicht so populär war. Mittlerweile hat ein Großteil der Gesellschaft verstanden, wie es funktioniert, oder hat zumindest schon davon gehört. Dadurch ist natürlich die Menge der veröffentlichten Bilder enorm gewachsen. Millionen von Menschen publizieren jeden Tag ihre Selbstporträts. Es entstehen so nebenbei immense Bildarchive mit echten Userbildern.*

[I] Diese große Menge an Bildern entstand auch, weil es heute viel einfacher ist, Bilder hochzuladen. Vor ein paar Jahren musste der Serviceprovider die Möglichkeit zum Hochladen zur Verfügung stellen. Es gab sogar eigens Firmen, die „Hochladesoftware" entwickelten. Heute ist in fast jedem Handy die entsprechende Software für den Nutzer mit einem Klick verfügbar. Bis das Bild meinen Freunden zugänglich ist, dauert es nur wenige Augenblicke. Diese Einfachheit des Vorgangs macht es dann aber auch leichter, jeglichen Content hochzuladen. Nicht nur eigene Bilder, sondern auch Bilder, die andere Menschen oder Marken zeigen. Dass damit Persönlichkeitsrechte oder Markenrechte verletzt werden, wissen viele Nutzer nicht. Auch dafür ist

abusive content had to be created together with the option to publish photos. Among other things, this protects minors and safeguards intellectual property rights and privacy. Today, these are the well-known "report user" and "report photo" links present in social networks. Reported content is dealt with by specially trained picture editors. This is a role which we also created in our company.

[P] *A few years ago there were relatively few photos as not many people had camera phones and public communication using images wasn't all that popular. In the meantime, the majority of people have come to understand how this works, or they are, at least, aware of it. Of course, this then led to a huge increase in the number of photographs being published. Millions of people upload their self-portraits on a daily basis. This has brought about the creation of extensive picture archives containing real user photos.*

[I] This huge number of images also emerged due to the increased simplicity of uploading pictures nowadays. A few years ago, users were reliant upon the service provider to give the option of uploading content. Companies even emerged which specifically developed "uploading software". Today, nearly all mobile phones are equipped with the relevant software which is accessible at the click of a button. It only takes a couple of seconds until friends can view my photo. The simplicity of this process, however, makes it even easier to upload all kinds of content. Not just your own pictures, but also pictures which show other people or brands. Many users are unaware of the fact that this actually infringes privacy or trademark rights – another example of why picture editors are needed.

[P] *I've always found it fascinating to see which photos are sometimes uploaded. As a picture editor, you quickly develop an eye for "strange" photos, that is conspicuous images, as you look at thousands of them every day. You come across*

eine Bildredaktion notwendig.

[P] *Ich fand es schon immer erstaunlich, welche Bilder teilweise hochgeladen werden. Als Bildredakteur hat man ziemlich schnell ein Auge für „komische", heißt auffällige Bilder, weil man täglich Tausende anschaut. Es wird von der privaten Hanfplantage im Wohnzimmer über tätowierte rechtsradikale Symbole bis hin zu Pornografie alles angeboten. Diese Inhalte werden in sozialen Netzwerken sehr schnell bemerkt und zensiert. Aber anscheinend besteht ein großer Reiz darin, anderen „verbotene Dinge" zu zeigen.*

[I] Die dann für immer im Internet zu finden sind! Vermutlich sind sich einige Leute nicht wirklich darüber bewusst, dass ein Veröffentlichen im Internet breiten Zugang zu einem Bild oder einer Information schaffen kann, der sich nicht so einfach rückgängig machen lässt. Der Wunsch nach Selbstdarstellung ist oft so groß, dass diese Überlegungen gar nicht gemacht werden oder in den Hintergrund treten. Auf der anderen Seite gibt es immer mehr Nutzer, die sehr darauf bedacht sind, was mit ihren Informationen passiert und wer dazu Zugang hat. Ich habe den Eindruck, dass sich hier gerade zwei Extreme entwickeln. Ein paar meiner Bekannten weigern sich, auch nur ein Profil anzulegen, andere nutzen das soziale Netzwerk als ihre private Bühne, bloggen ihr ganzes Leben in Bildern und Statusmeldungen, vom Frühstück bis zum Schlafengehen – was sie dazu antreibt, kann ich oft nur vermuten. Dieses Phänomen zu sehen und zu erkennen, hat uns auf die Idee mit dem Buch gebracht.

[P] *Ja, das Phänomen der Social Network Photography ist zwar relativ neu, aber schon global verbreitet. Zu Anfang unseres Buchprojekts sammelte ich Bilder, die mir in irgendeiner Form interessant oder besonders schienen. Wobei ein schlechtes Foto durchaus ein gutes Bild sein kann. Auffällig war, dass sich bestimmte Themen und Posen weltweit wiederholten. Sujets öfter*

everything from private, living-room cannabis farms and tattoos of right-wing symbols to pornography. This type of content is detected and censored extremely quickly in social networks. However, there seems to be quite an attraction to sharing "prohibited things".

[I] Which are then saved to the Internet forever! It would seem that not all people are quite aware that publishing something on the Internet can create wide access to a picture or information, which is then very hard to undo. The desire for self-portrayal is often so huge that these aspects are either not even considered or simply swept aside. On the other hand, there are more and more users who are extremely anxious about what will happen to their information and who will be able to access it. I get the feeling that there are two extremities at work here. A few people I know are apprehensive of even creating a profile, whereas others use social networks as their private stage, blogging their entire lives through pictures and status updates from breakfast to bedtime – more often than not I can only guess at what drives them to do this. Seeing and recognising this phenomenon brought us to the idea of putting together this book.

[P] *Yes, the Social Network Photography phenomenon is relatively new, but it has already caught on all around the world. When we started our book project I began collecting photos which I found interesting in some way or which particularly stood out. That isn't to say that a bad photo can't be a good image. It was remarkable to see that certain themes and poses repeated themselves on a global scale. Motifs often recurred. With this in mind, I began to sort the photos according to different categories, which later became the book's different chapters. As all the photos were taken on mobile phones, the picture quality is sometimes rather pixelated due to the low resolution. However, this is what makes them*

auftauchten. Daraufhin begann ich, die Bildersammlung nach verschiedenen Kategorien zu sortieren, aus denen später die Buchkapitel entstanden. Da alle Fotos mit Handykameras aufgenommen wurden, ist die Bildqualität durch deren niedrige Auflösung zum Teil entsprechend pixelig. Genau das macht die Fotos aber aus, definiert sie als echt. Ein weiteres signifikantes Merkmal vieler Bilder, neben der „roughen", verzogenen Optik und Unschärfe, sind die teilweise skurrilen Orte und Situationen, in denen sie aufgenommen wurden. Beispielsweise beim „Toilet-" oder „Bathroom-Shot", der entsteht, weil der benötigte Spiegel sich zumeist im Badezimmer oder auch auf öffentlichen Toiletten befindet. So ist dann unweigerlich viel mehr auf dem Bild drauf, als wahrscheinlich beabsichtigt war.

[I] Mir scheint, dass man, anders als bei Fotos, die im Fotostudio vor einer dunkelbraunen Wand aufgenommen werden, aus diesen Selbstporträts ziemlich viel über die einzelnen Personen erfahren kann.

[P] *Fast alle Fotos erzählen sehr private Geschichten über die Lebensumstände, aber auch das persönliche Umfeld ihrer Autoren. Sie geben gleichzeitig einen Einblick in den Stand der heutigen Gesellschaft, deren Zeitgeist. Auf Bildern aus den unterschiedlichsten Teilen der Welt sieht man Gemeinsamkeiten der Fotografierenden, in ihren Styles, ihrer Kleidung und ihren Gesten. Ich habe gelernt: Es gibt Emos auf den Philippinen. Manche argentinischen Mädchen lieben Japan-Rock. In anderen Breitengraden ist ein Zimmerventilator von Vorteil. Wäre ich Britin, dann wäre ich wahrscheinlich schon als Teenager ungewollt schwanger geworden. Und Männer laden ein Bild ihres Penis hoch, um Kontakte zu knüpfen.*

[I] Tatsächlich scheint das mit den Kontakten ja zu klappen. Wahrscheinlich nicht mit solchen Bildern, aber wir wissen, dass sich zum Beispiel schon Paare gefunden haben, aber auch getrennt. Und einen itsmy-Nachwuchs gibt es auch schon.

interesting and defines them as being authentic. Another significant feature of many of the photos, apart from the "rough" distorted look and blurriness, is the sometimes bizarre locations and situations in which they were taken. For example, the toilet or bathroom shot which has evolved due to the required mirror normally being found in the bathroom or public toilets. This means that the picture inevitably ends up showing much more than was probably intended.

[I] *I find that you can tell a lot about people's individual characteristics from these self-pottraits, compared with a photo taken in a professional studio in front of a dark background.*

[P] *Almost all the photos tell very private stories, not only about the subject's living conditions, but also about their personal environment. At the same time, they also give an insight into society as it stands today, its "zeitgeist". Despite the photos originating from all corners of the world, there are still similarities in terms of their subjects — be it in their style, clothing or gestures. This project has taught me a few things: there are emos in the Philippines; some Argentinean girls love Japanese rock; having a fan in your room is an asset if you live along certain latitudinal lines; were I British, I would have probably gotten unintentionally pregnant as a teenager; and men upload a photo of their penis to help them establish contacts.*

[I] *The establishing contacts element really does seem to work. Probably not with those types of pictures, but we do know, for example, that couples have both formed and split up. And there has already been an itsmy baby. The parents' request to call their child itsmy was, however, rejected by the authorities. What goes on in a social network is always extremely personal. Many people want to express things about themselves, their opinions, their philosophies of life or their emotions to their friends, their circle. Can this be achieved through photos?*

[P] *Here and there I discovered extremely personal*

Der Wunsch der Eltern, das Kind itsmy zu nennen, wurde allerdings von den Behörden abgelehnt. Was sich in einem sozialen Netzwerk abspielt, ist immer sehr nahe am Einzelnen. Viele wollen ihren Freunden, ihrer Umwelt etwas über sich, ihre Meinung, ihre Weltanschauung oder ihre Stimmung mitteilen. Auch mittels der Bilder?

[P] *Vereinzelt entdeckte ich sehr persönliche Bildwelten, die etwas erzählen, was über die gekonnte Selbstinszenierung hinausging. Bilder, in denen ihre Macher eine eigene Sicht formulieren. Direkt. Echt. Privat. Teilweise so nah, als wäre man selbst mit dabei. Aufgenommen mit einer eigenen Bildsprache und Originalität, einem sehr ausgeprägten individuellen, persönlichen Stil, der exemplarisch für das ganze Phänomen der Selbstdarstellungsfotografie in sozialen Netzwerken stehen kann. Deshalb haben wir uns diesen Personen im Buch etwas ausführlicher gewidmet.*

[I] Ohne all diejenigen, die sich mit Freude und Enthusiasmus dem Selbstporträt widmen, wäre dieses Buch nicht möglich gewesen. Aus der Masse von Abertausenden von Bildern aus sozialen Netzwerken, Profilen bei Facebook, itsmy, aber auch Twitter stachen einige Bilder regelrecht heraus. Wir haben diese Fotos von Nutzern aus der ganzen Welt zur Verfügung gestellt bekommen, um mit unserem Buch einen Überblick über Fotografie in sozialen Netzwerken zu geben und diese neue Form der Kommunikation und der Kunst einem breiten Publikum vorzustellen.

Für all unsere Leser haben wir eine Facebook-Seite erstellt. Wir freuen uns auf Meinungen, Fotos und Geschichten aus der ganzen Welt.
www.facebook.com/socialnetworkphotography

pictorial worlds which expressed something that went beyond the skill of self-staging. Pictures, whose creators illustrate their views. Direct. Authentic. Private. Sometimes so close, it's as if you're part of them. Incorporating unique visual language and originality, an extremely distinctive, individual personal style, which is exemplary of the entire phenomenon of self portrayal photography in social networks. This is why we chose to specifically feature these people in our book.

[I] The book wouldn't have been possible without all those who devote so much joy and enthusiasm to the self-portrait. There were a few photos which really stood out from the thousands upon thousands of pictures in social networks, Facebook, itsmy, and even Twitter profiles. Users across the globe have given us access to these photos in order to allow our book both to give an overview of the type of photography found in social-networks and to present this new form of communication and art to a wider audience.

We have created a Facebook page for all our readers. We look forward to receiving your opinions, photos and stories from all over the world.
www.facebook.com/socialnetworkphotography

Ich fotografiere mich selbst. Jederzeit und an jedem Ort. Mit einer Hand. Oder mit beiden. Die einzige Grenze ist die Länge des Arms.

I take pictures of myself. Whenever and wherever. With one hand. Or with both. The only restriction is the length of my arm.

ARM'S LENGTH

ONE HANDED

21 years, Argentina

ARM'S LENGTH - ONE HANDED

31 years, France

29 years, UK

ARM'S LENGTH - ONE HANDED

19 years, Mexico

22 years, Swaziland

ARM'S LENGTH - ONE HANDED

23 years, USA

ARM'S LENGTH - ONE HANDED

26 years, Mexico

20 years, UK

ARM'S LENGTH - ONE HANDED

18 years, Nigeria

33 years, India

ARM'S LENGTH - ONE HANDED

TWO HANDED

27 years, Philippines

25 years, Ireland

ARM'S LENGTH - TWO HANDED

ARM IN SUNGLASSES

26 years, USA

ARM'S LENGTH – ARM IN SUNGLASSES

24 years, South Africa

ARM'S LENGTH - ARM IN SUNGLASSES — 27 years, South Africa

20 years, India

ARM'S LENGTH - ARM IN SUNGLASSES

20 years, Philippines

24 years, South Africa

ARM'S LENGTH - ARM IN SUNGLASSES

24 years, Nigeria

23 years, Namibia

ARM'S LENGTH - ARM IN SUNGLASSES

18 years, Costa Rica

ARM'S LENGTH - ARM IN SUNGLASSES

Ich im Spiegel. Die einfachste Form, sich selbst zu fotografieren. Meist im heimischen Bad oder auf öffentlichen Toiletten. Braucht etwas Übung. Könner schaffen es, das Handy nicht vor das Gesicht zu halten.

Me in the mirror. The easiest way to take a picture myself. Usually in my bathroom or in public toilets. Takes some practice. Pros manage not to cover their face with their phone.

ME IN THE MIRROR

FACE COVERED

24 years, Uruguay

ME IN THE MIRROR - FACE COVERED

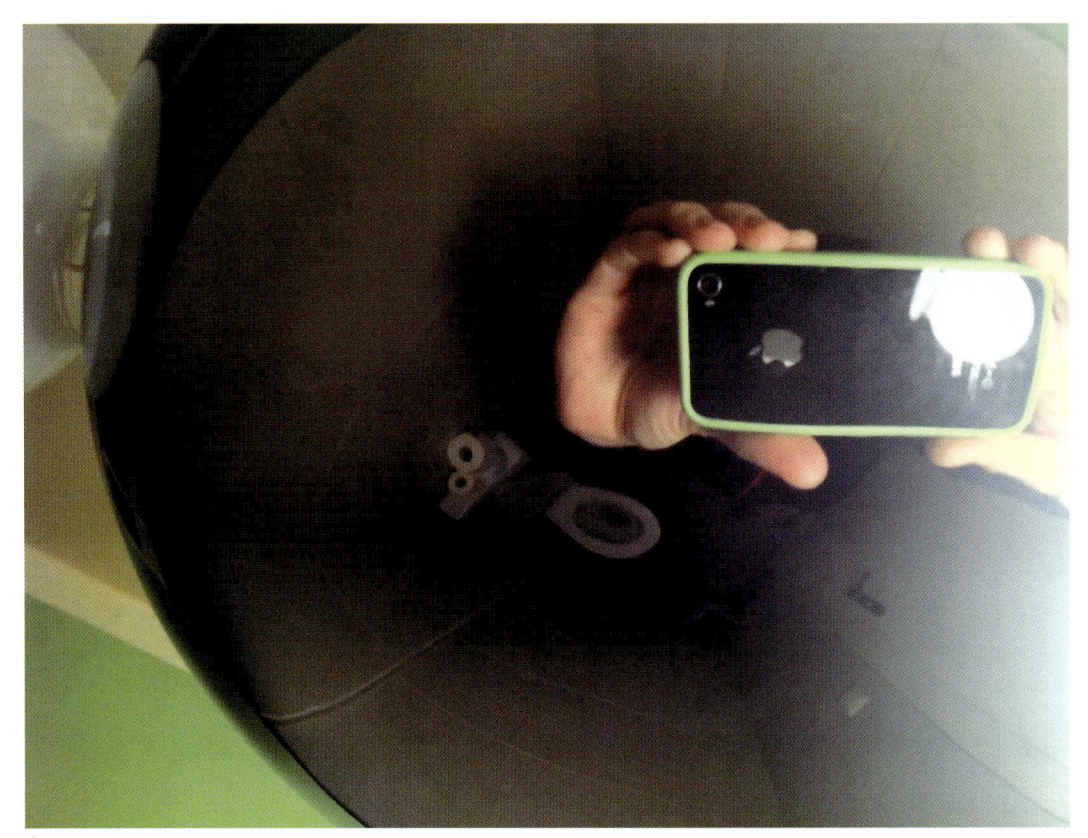

41 years, Austria

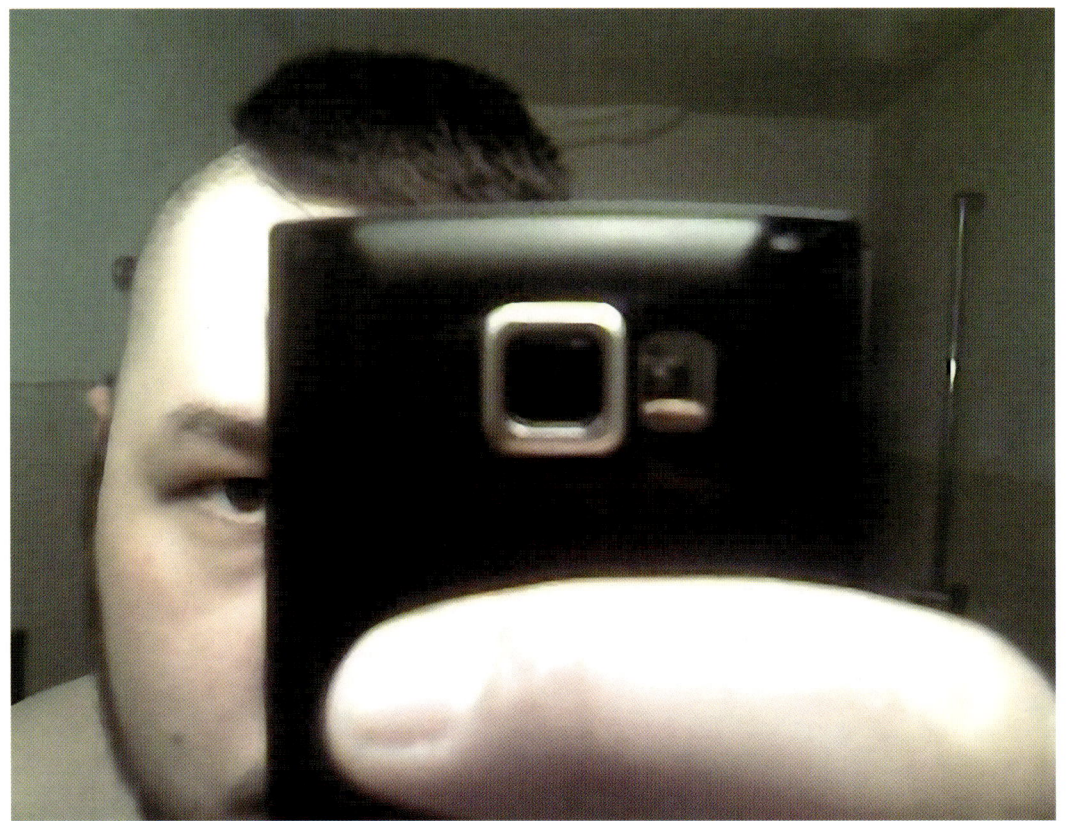

34 years, Germany

20 years, Guatemala

ME IN THE MIRROR - FACE COVERED

21 years, Kenya

23 years, Nigeria

ME IN THE MIRROR - FACE COVERED

25 years, USA

ME IN THE MIRROR - FACE COVERED

20 years, UK

CAMERA CHECK

25 years, USA

ME IN THE MIRROR - CAMERA CHECK

24 years, UK

24 years, UK

24 years, UK

24 years, UK

24 years, UK

ME IN THE MIRROR - CAMERA CHECK

19 years, UK

ME IN THE MIRROR - CAMERA CHECK

27 years, USA

23 years, USA

18 years, Brazil

27 years, USA

ME IN THE MIRROR - CAMERA CHECK

24 years, Nigeria

ME IN THE MIRROR - CAMERA CHECK   20 years, Italy

MIRROR SHAPES

20 years, Nigeria

ME IN THE MIRROR - MIRROR SHAPES

35 years, USA

27 years, Namibia

24 years, UK

24 years, Paraguay

ME IN THE MIRROR - MIRROR SHAPES

27 years, USA

34 years, Finland

ME IN THE MIRROR - MIRROR SHAPES

23 years, Nigeria

25 years, USA

ME IN THE MIRROR - MIRROR SHAPES

PROS

40 years, UK

ME IN THE MIRROR - PROS

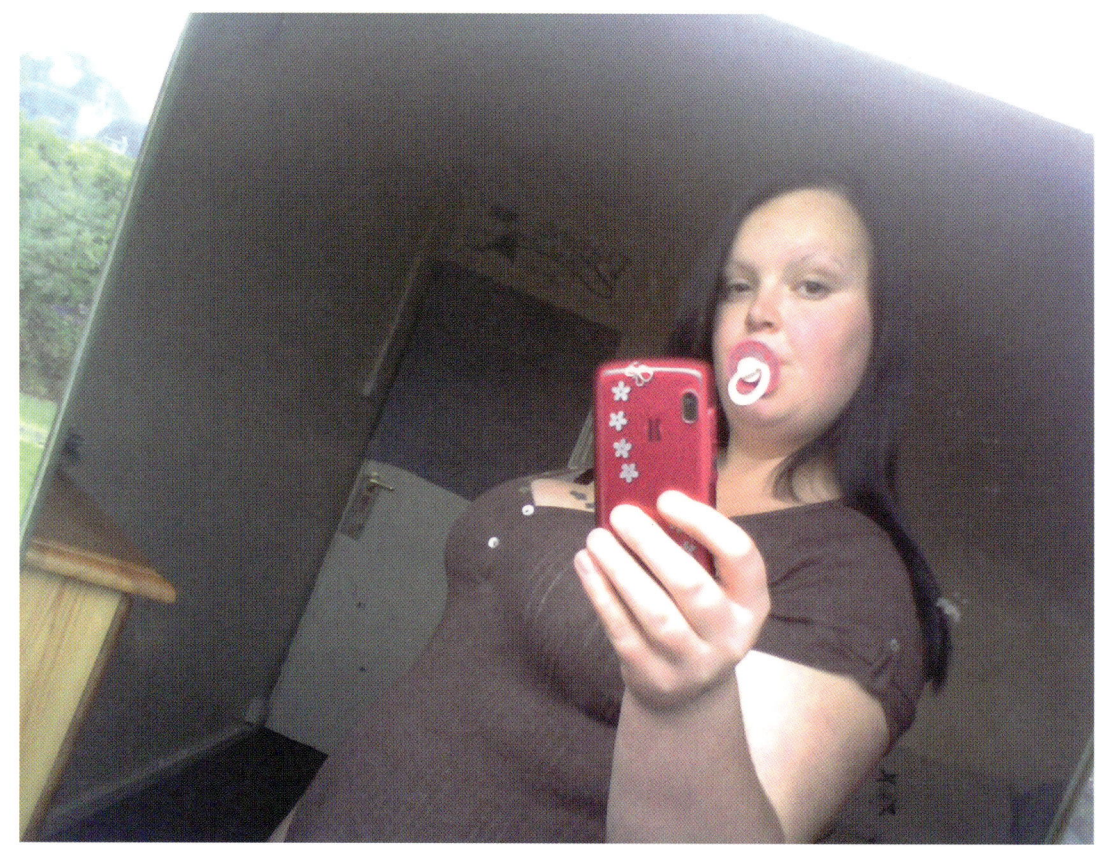

19 years, UK

18 years, UK

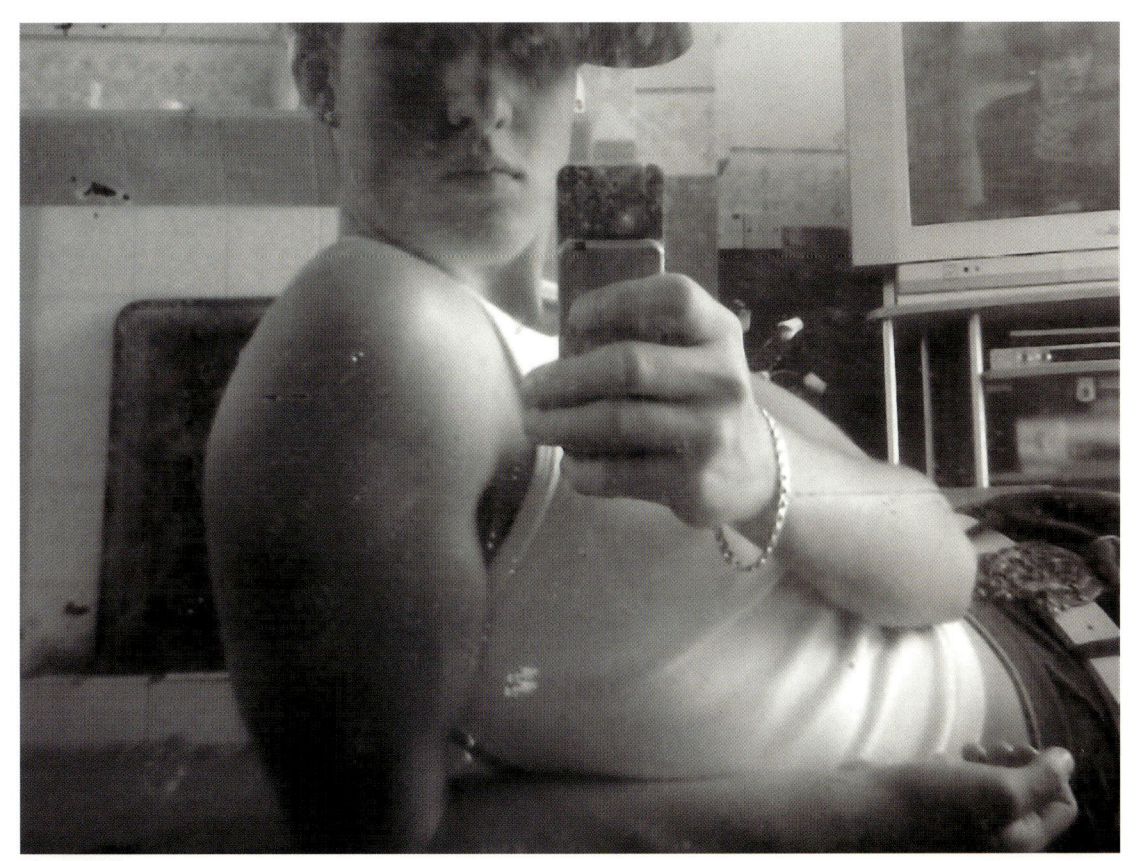

18 years, UK

28 years, Sweden

ME IN THE MIRROR - PROS

31 years, USA

ME IN THE MIRROR - PROS   25 years, USA

18 years, UK

30 years, Guatemala

ME IN THE MIRROR - PROS

ME IN THE MIRROR - PROS   21 years, India

24 years, USA

23 years, USA

ME IN THE MIRROR - PROS

Überall auf der Welt haben Menschen ihre Handykameras immer dabei und gewähren mit zahlreichen Fotos fortwährend Einblick in ihr persönliches Umfeld.

Ich. Zu Hause. In meiner Umgebung. Bei der Arbeit. Unterwegs.

All around the world, people always have their camera phones to hand. Photo after photo they provide us with constant insights into their personal surroundings.

Me. At home. In my surroundings. At work. On the road.

LOCATION

SURROUNDINGS

33 years, South Africa

LOCATION - SURROUNDINGS

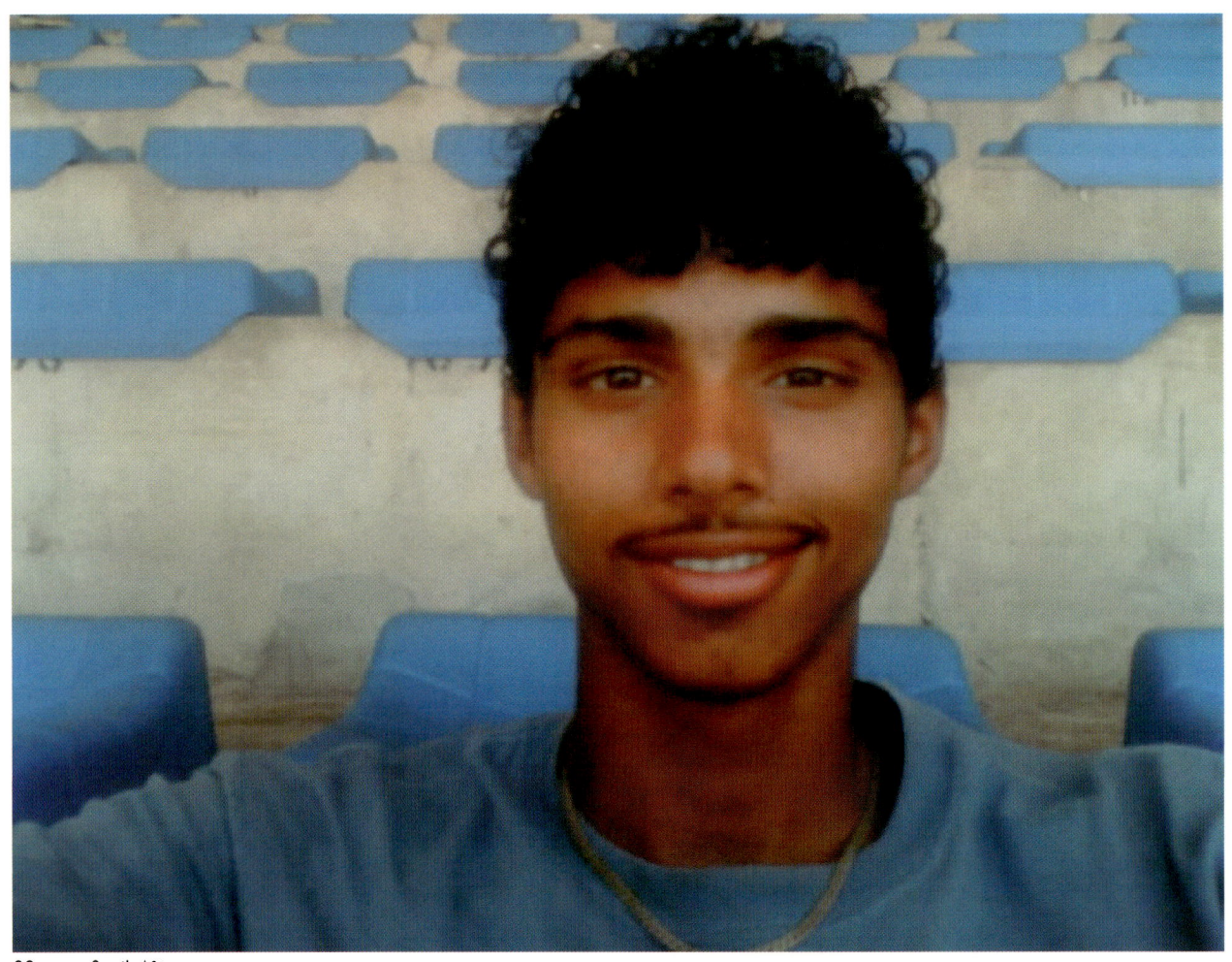

22 years, South Africa

30 years, Romania

21 years, Indonesia

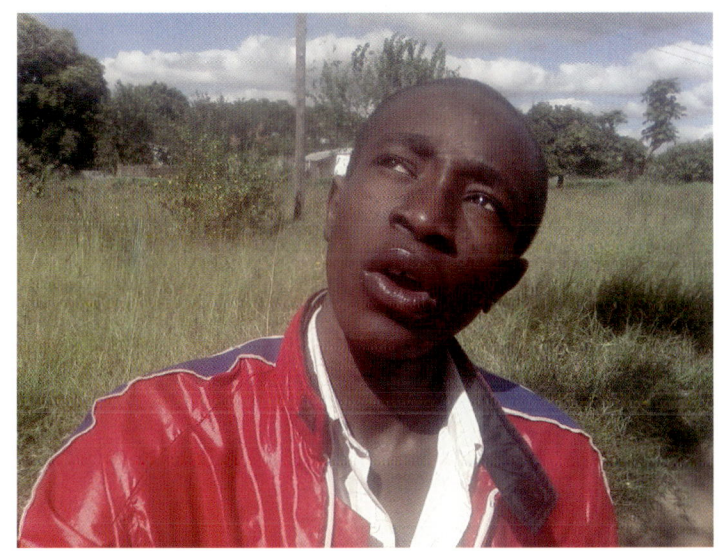

21 years, Zambia

LOCATION - SURROUNDINGS

25 years, South Africa

46 years, Indonesia

LOCATION - SURROUNDINGS

33 years, Thailand

LOCATION - Surroundings   26 years, Pakistan

26 years, Nigeria

18 years, Nigeria

28 years, Pakistan

23 years, Nigeria

27 years, Nigeria

21 years, Venezuela

LOCATION - SURROUNDINGS

22 years, Zambia

LOCATION - SURROUNDINGS

33 years, UK

LOCATION - SURROUNDINGS

23 years, India

LOCATION - SURROUNDINGS

MY ROOM

39 years, Indonesia

LOCATION - MY ROOM

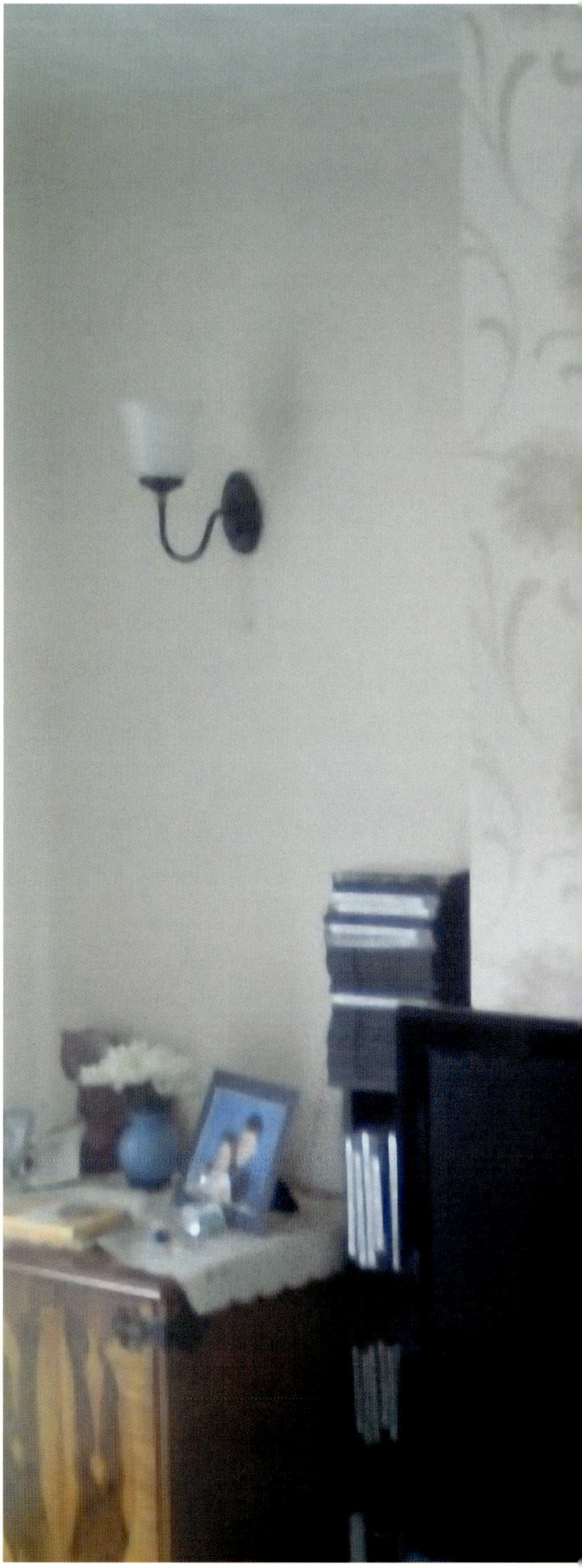

26 years, UK

LOCATION - MY ROOM

21 years, Namibia

25 years, India

LOCATION - MY ROOM

25 years, Ireland

LOCATION - MY ROOM

23 years, Nigeria

LOCATION - MY ROOM

MY PROFESSION

21 years, Mozambique

LOCATION - MY PROFESSION

29 years, South Africa

LOCATION - MY PROFESSION

ON THE ROAD

23 years, USA

LOCATION - ON THE ROAD

26 years, USA

37 years, Italy

LOCATION - ON THE ROAD

23 years, India

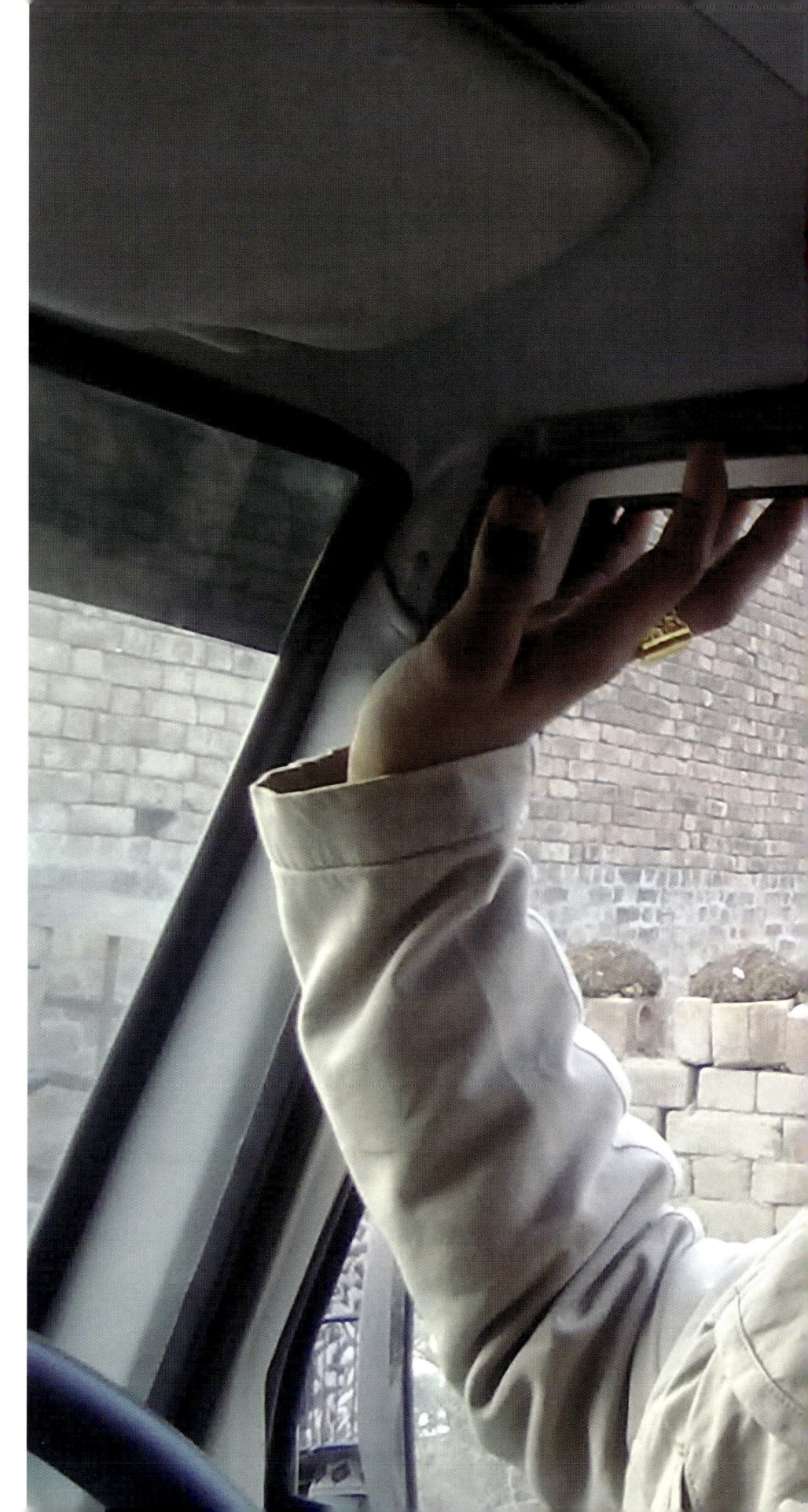

LOCATION - ON THE ROAD

Bilder in sozialen Netzwerken bedeuten Kommunikation. Sie personalisieren Nachrichten oder beweisen die Echtheit der Person.

Ich als Nachricht. Kommunikation durch Symbole. Texte. Zeichen.

Pictures in social networks symbolise communication. They personify messages or vouch for a person's authenticity.

Me as a message. Communicating through symbols. Texts. Signals.

MESSAGES

LOVE

Bianconiglia

20 years, Italy

MESSAGES - LOVE

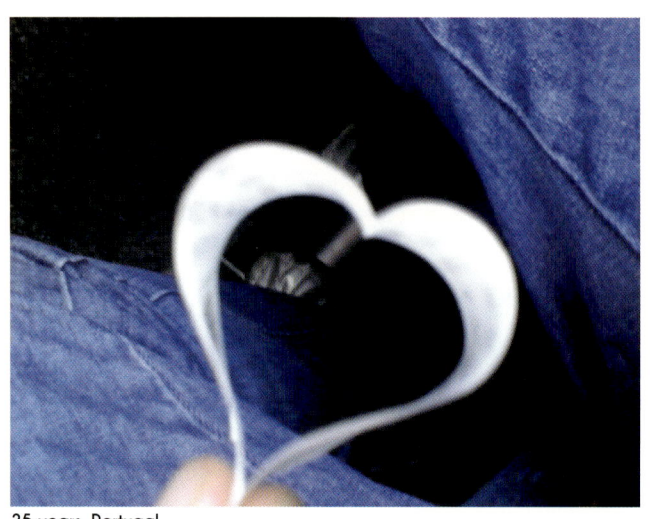

25 years, Portugal

28 years, UK

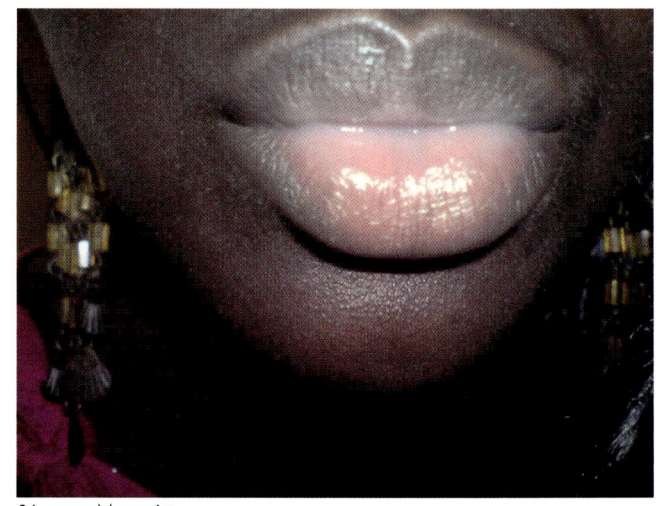

24 years, Indonesia

21 years, Mozambique

MESSAGES - LOVE   20 years, UK

AUTHENTICITY

27 years, South Africa

MESSAGES - AUTHENTICITY

23 years, Germany

27 years, Puerto Rico

23 years, USA

18 years, Mexico

20 years, Germany

23 years, Germany

MESSAGES - AUTHENTICITY

20 years, Germany

23 years, USA

MESSAGES - AUTHENTICITY

HAND GESTURES

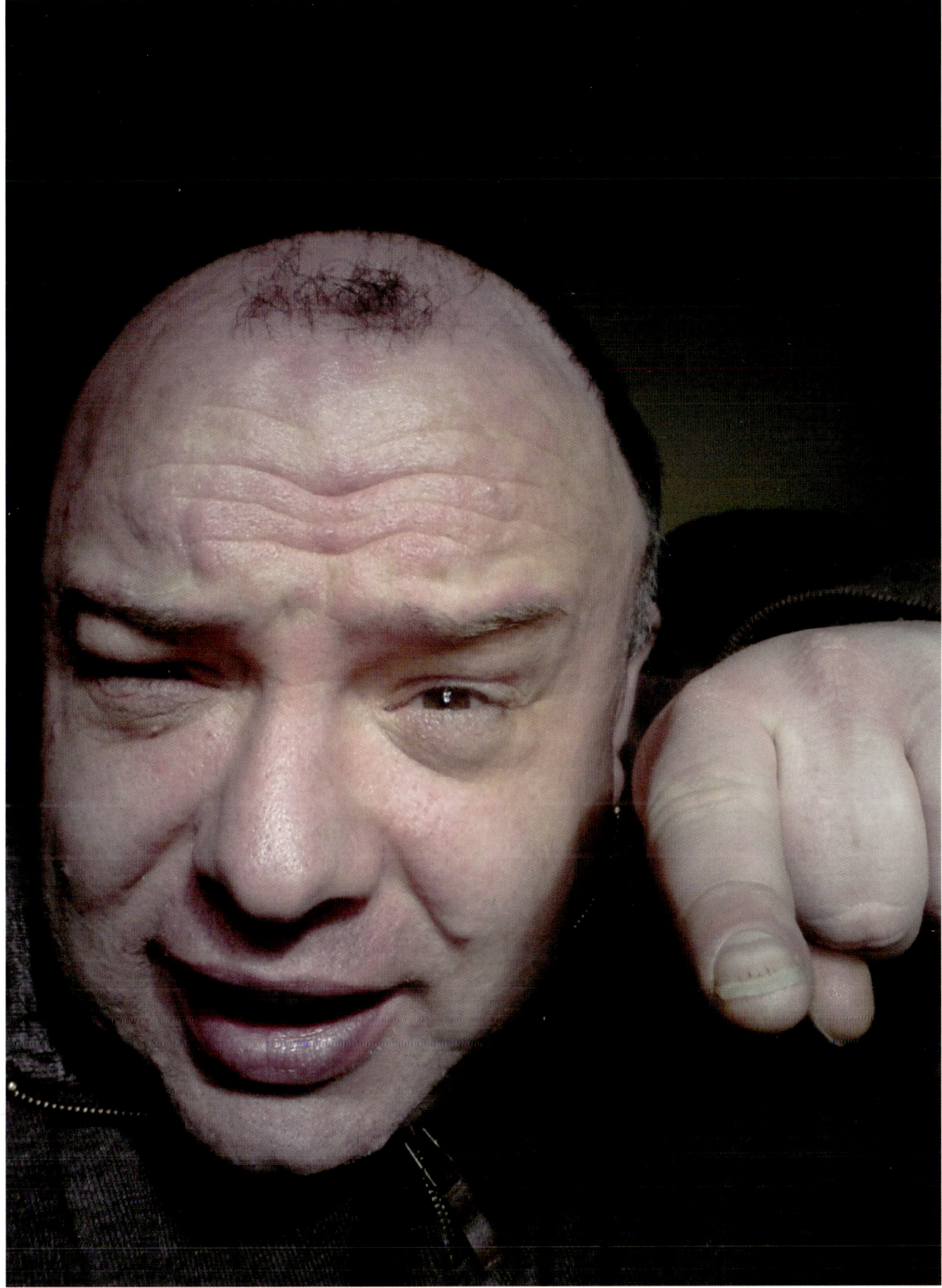

42 years, UK

MESSAGES - HAND GESTURES

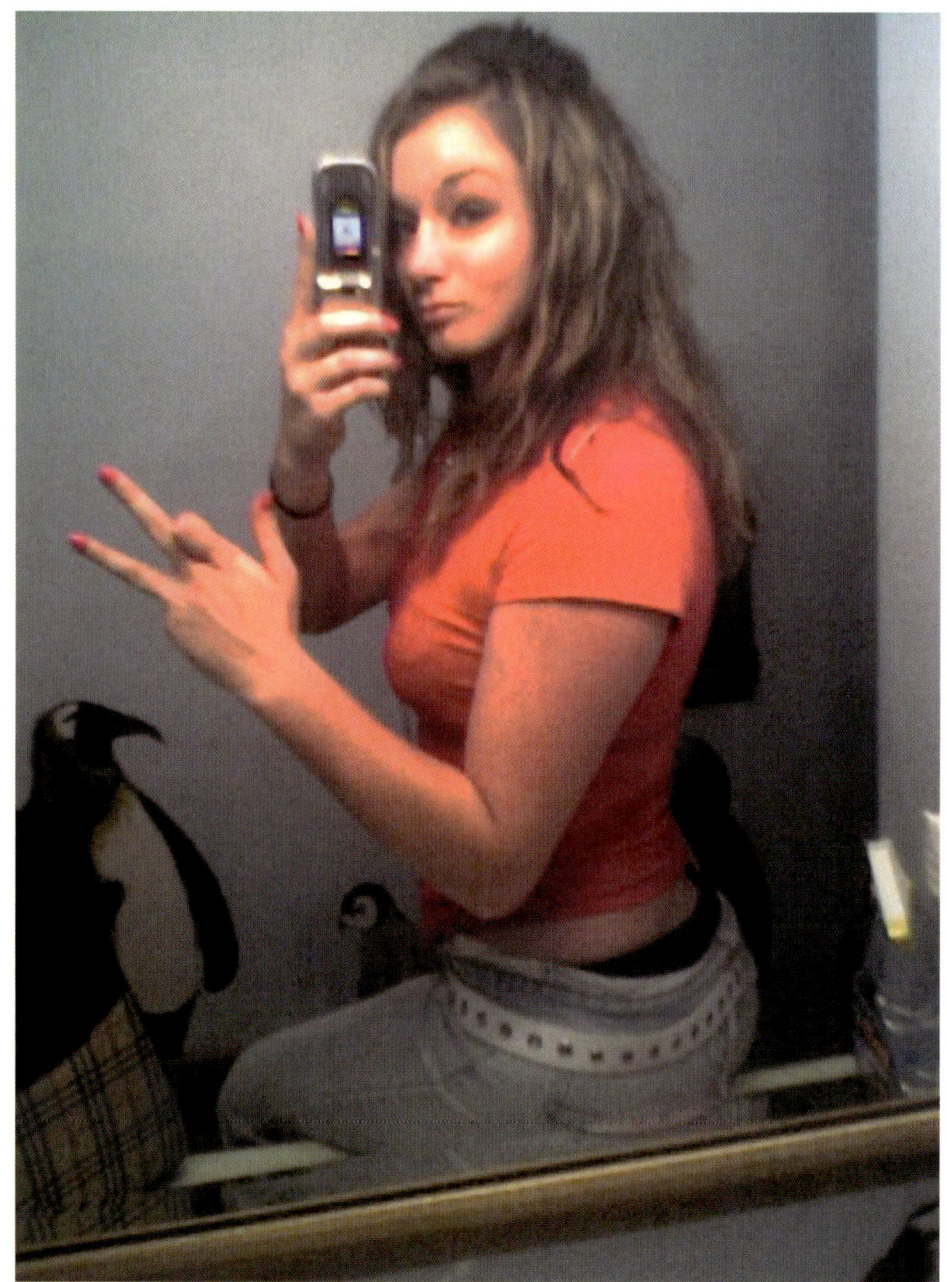

23 years, USA

27 years, Mexico

MESSAGES - HAND GESTURES

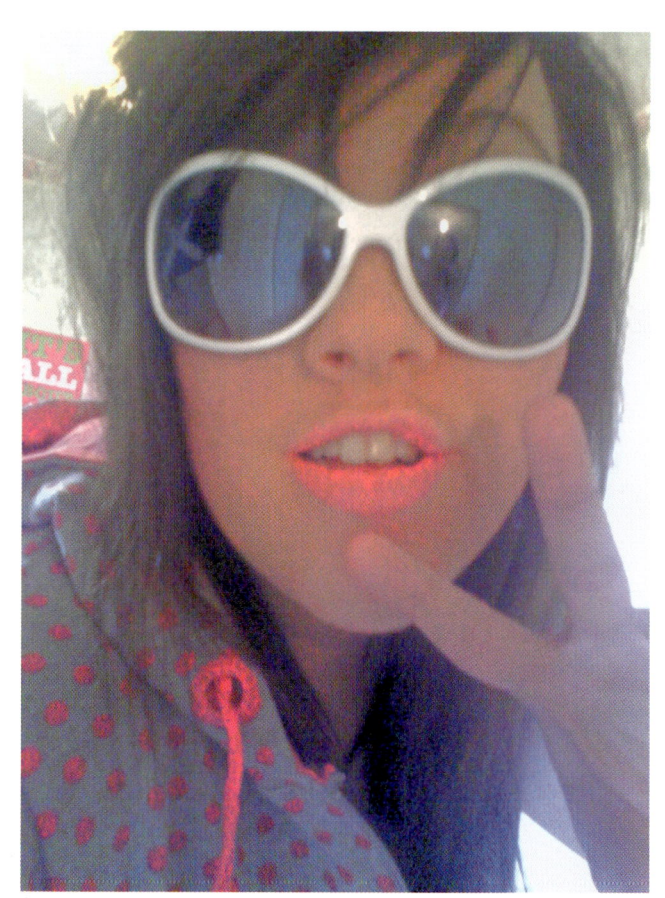

20 years, Guatemala

20 years, UK

21 years, Argentina

20 years, Guatemala

MESSAGES - HAND GESTURES

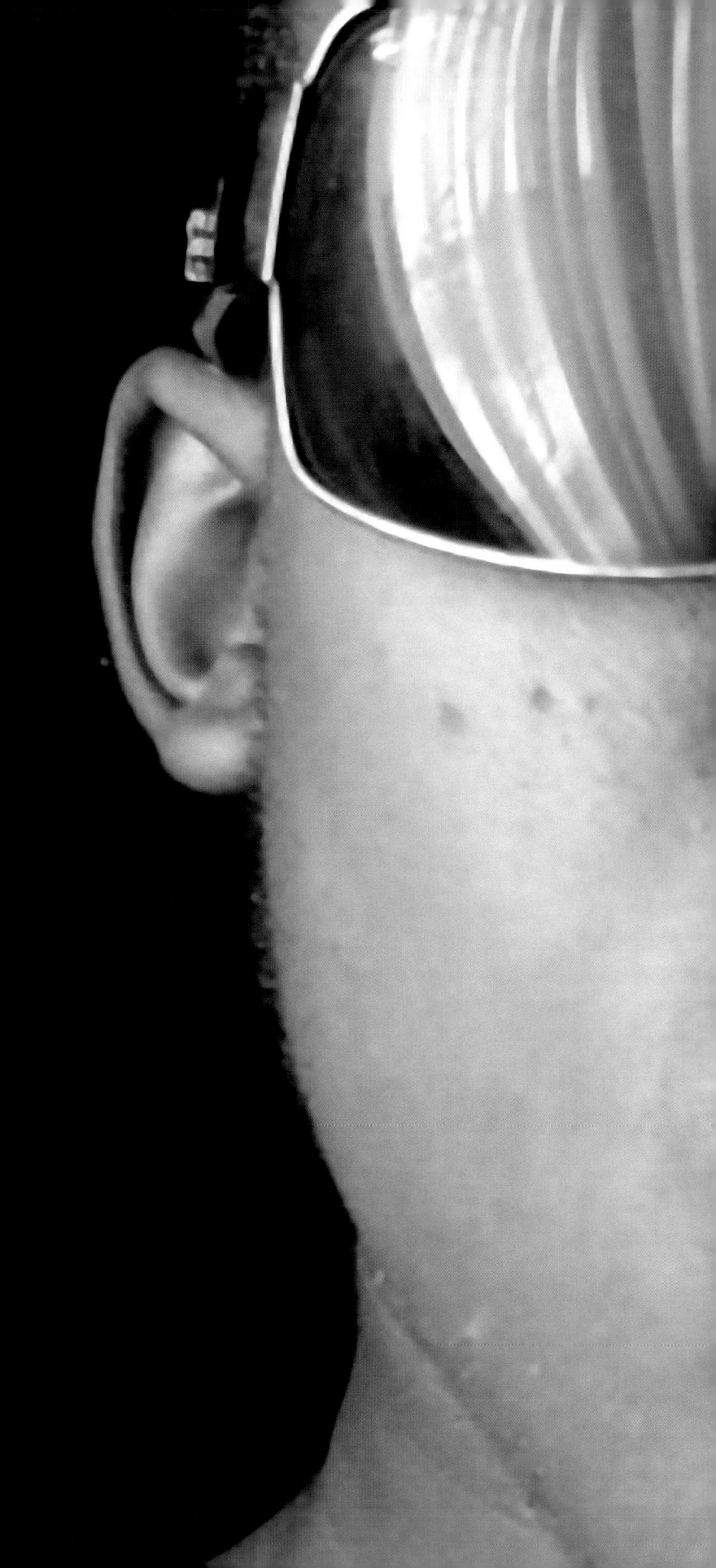

20 years, South Africa

MESSAGES - HAND GESTURES

Selbstinszenierung im Selbstporträt.
Mein Stil. Meine Pose.

Self-staging through self-portrait.
My style. My pose.

STYLEZ

MY STYLE

21 years, Nigeria

STYLEZ - MY STYLE

23 years, Zambia

STYLEZ - MY STYLE

36 years, South Africa

STYLEZ - MY STYLE

25 years, Zambia

19 years, Nigeria

21 years, Namibia

27 years, Ireland

32 years, India

30 years, Anguilla

27 years, Nigeria

26 years, Nigeria

20 years, South Africa

21 years, Namibia

STYLEZ - MY STYLE

20 years, UK

24 years, Uruguay

Just barsyl

20 years, Nigeria

STYLEZ - MY STYLE

23 years, USA

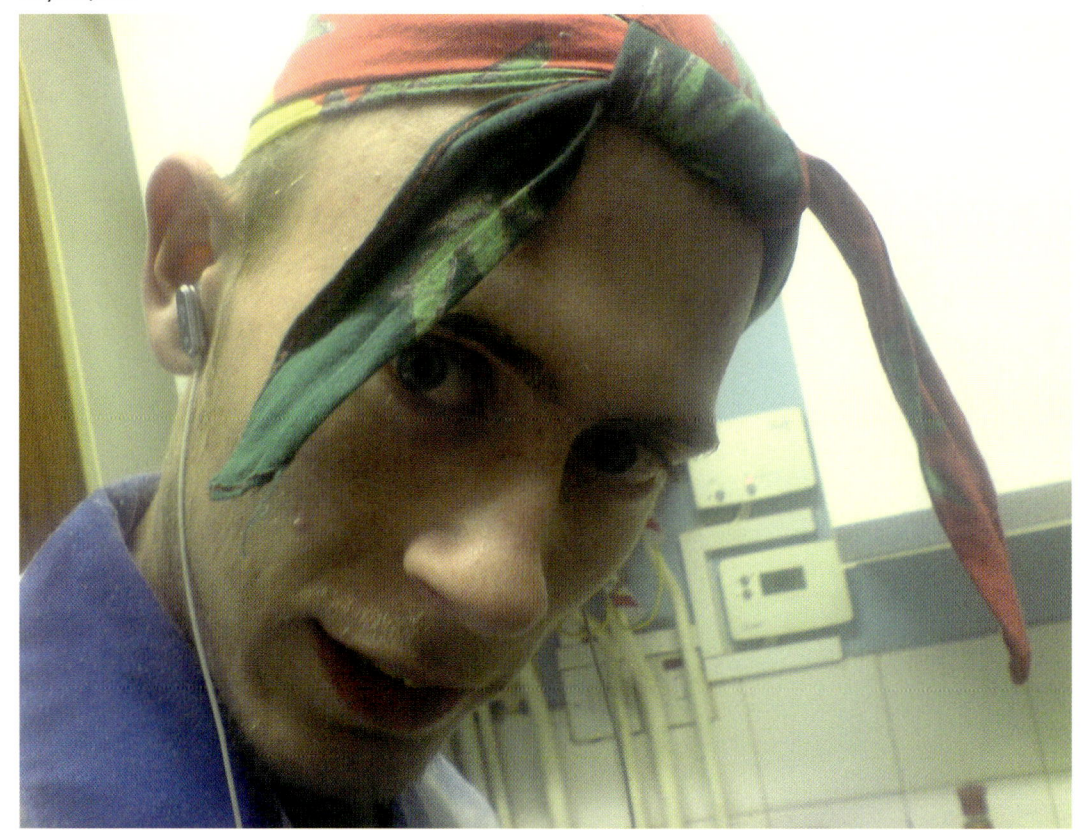

21 years, UK

22 years, Swaziland

22 years, Swaziland

STYLEZ - MY STYLE

27 years, Indonesia

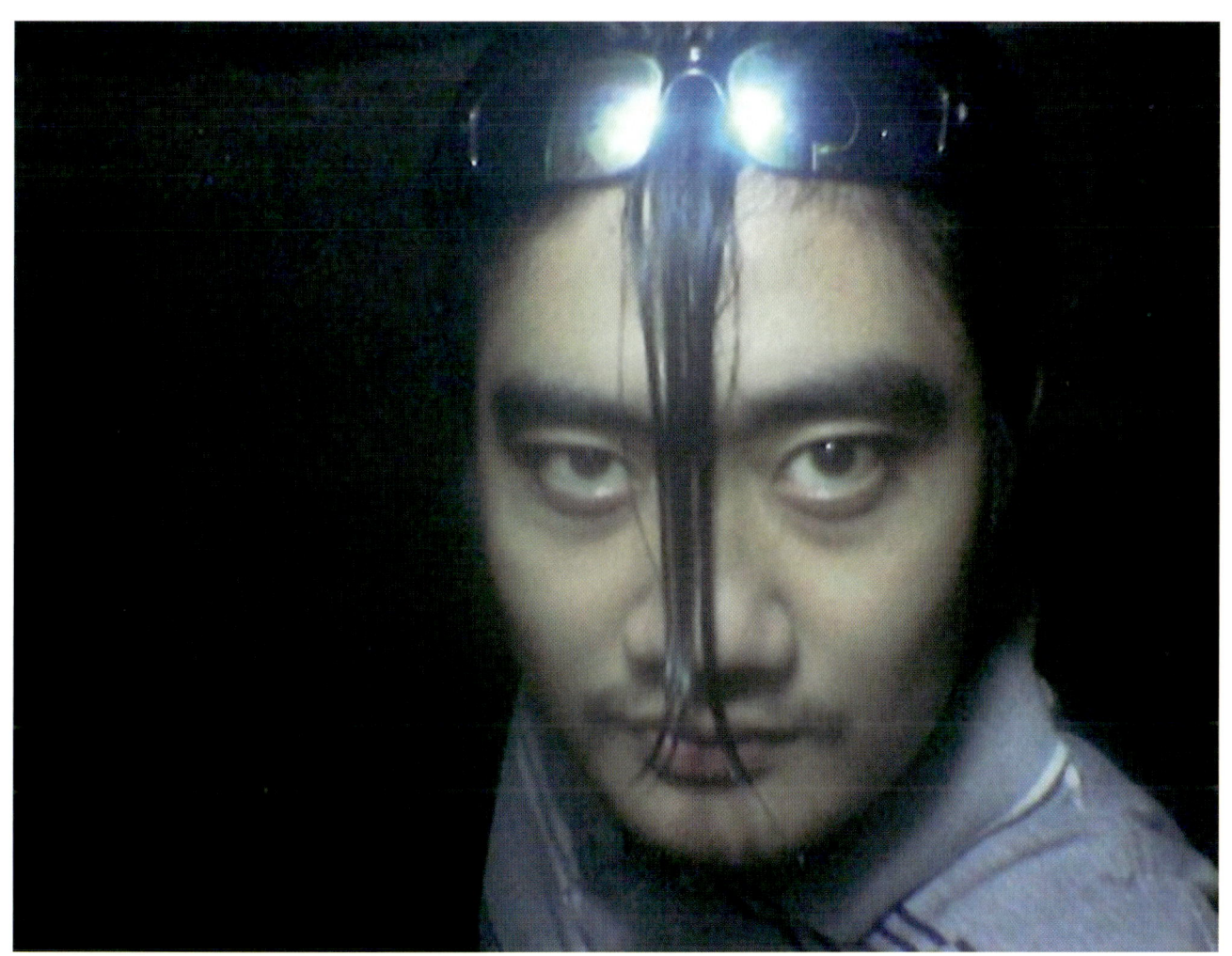

24 years, Indonesia

STYLEZ - MY STYLE

19 years, Mexico

31 years, France

STYLEZ - MY STYLE

MY TATTOO

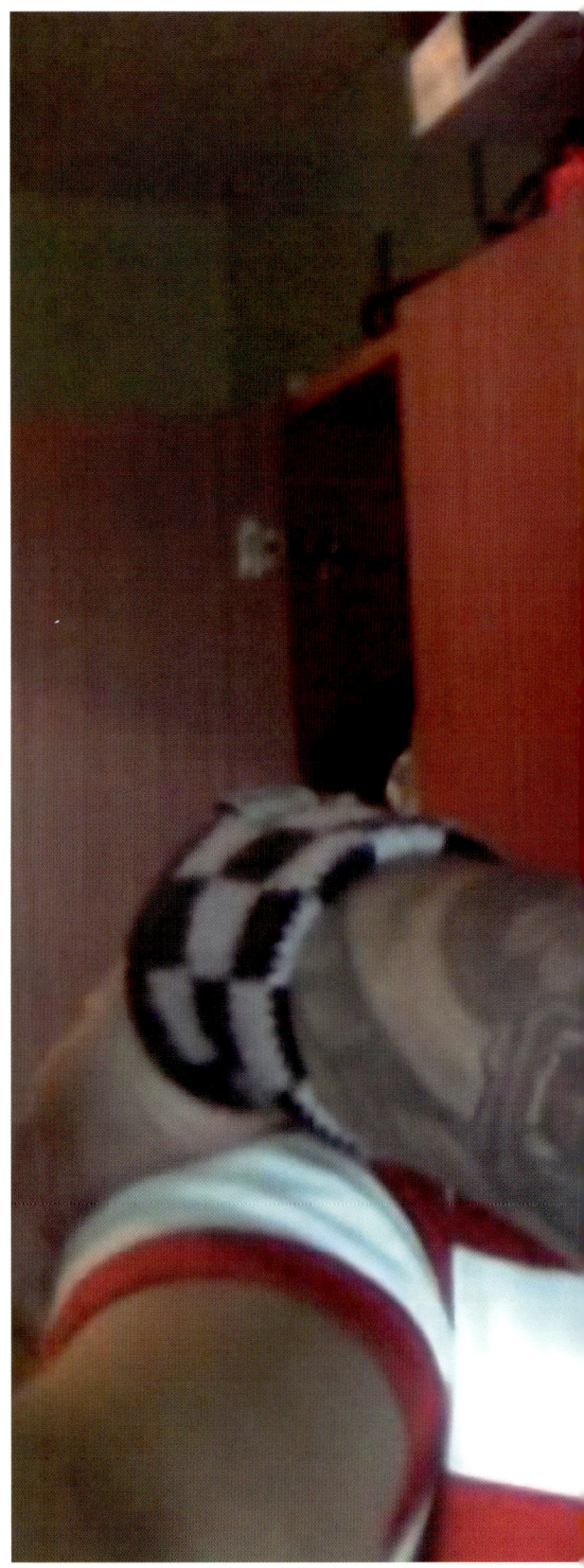

28 years, Argentina

STYLEZ - MY TATTOO

21 years, Guatemala

STYLEZ - MY TATTOO

Alltägliche Dinge oder besondere Situationen sind es wert, sofort mitgeteilt zu werden.

Mein Essen. Mein Haustier. Mein Schmuck. Meine liebsten Sachen.

Everyday objects or particular situations are worthy of being communicated at once.

My meal. My pet. My jewellery. My favourite things.

STUFF

MY STUFF

20 years, UK

STUFF - MY STUFF

25 years, Japan

25 years, Japan

21 years, Swaziland

28 years, Republic of Korea

18 years, Nigeria

27 years, USA

28 years, Republic of Korea

32 years, Australia

20 years, UK

Every true
Man knows
His worth

33 years, India

STUFF - MY STUFF

20 years, UK

MY MEAL

22 years, Indonesia

STUFF - MY MEAL

20 years, India

20 years, Moldova · STUFF - MY MEAL

25 years, India

24 years, Indonesia

36 years, USA

50 years, Puerto Rico

36 years, USA

STUFF - MY MEAL

30 years, UK

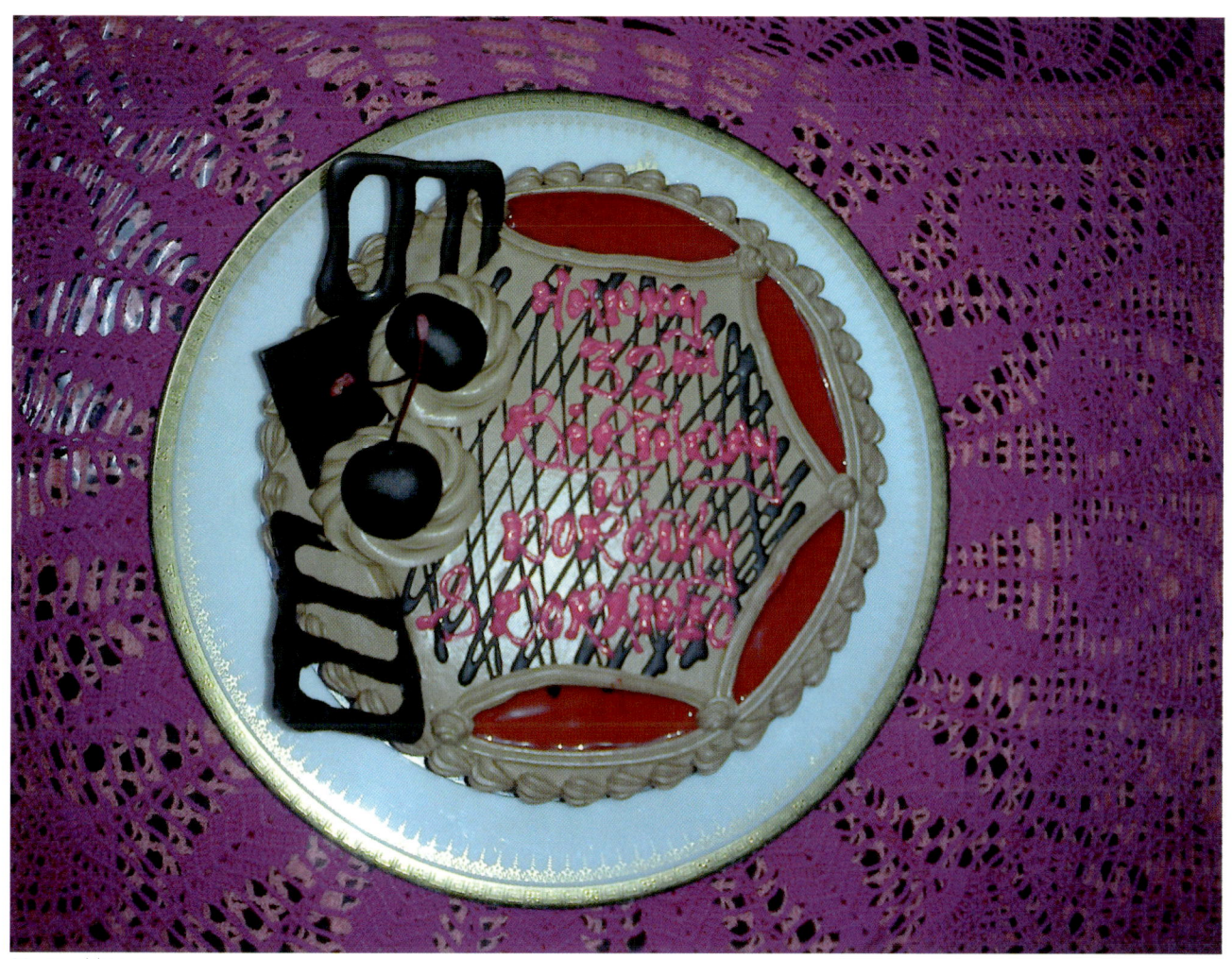

32 years, Malaysia

STUFF - MY MEAL

ME & MY PET

26 years, USA

27 years, Puerto Rico

STUFF - ME & MY PET

35 years, Australia

STUFF - ME & MY PET

22 years, Germany

26 years, USA

STUFF - ME & MY PET

Ich mache mein Bild noch schöner. I'll make my picture even better.
Sticker. Rahmen. Szenen. Stickers. Frames. Scenes.

PICTURE ENHANCEMENTS

24 years, USA

PICTURE ENHANCEMENTS

25 years, Japan

29 years, Kenya

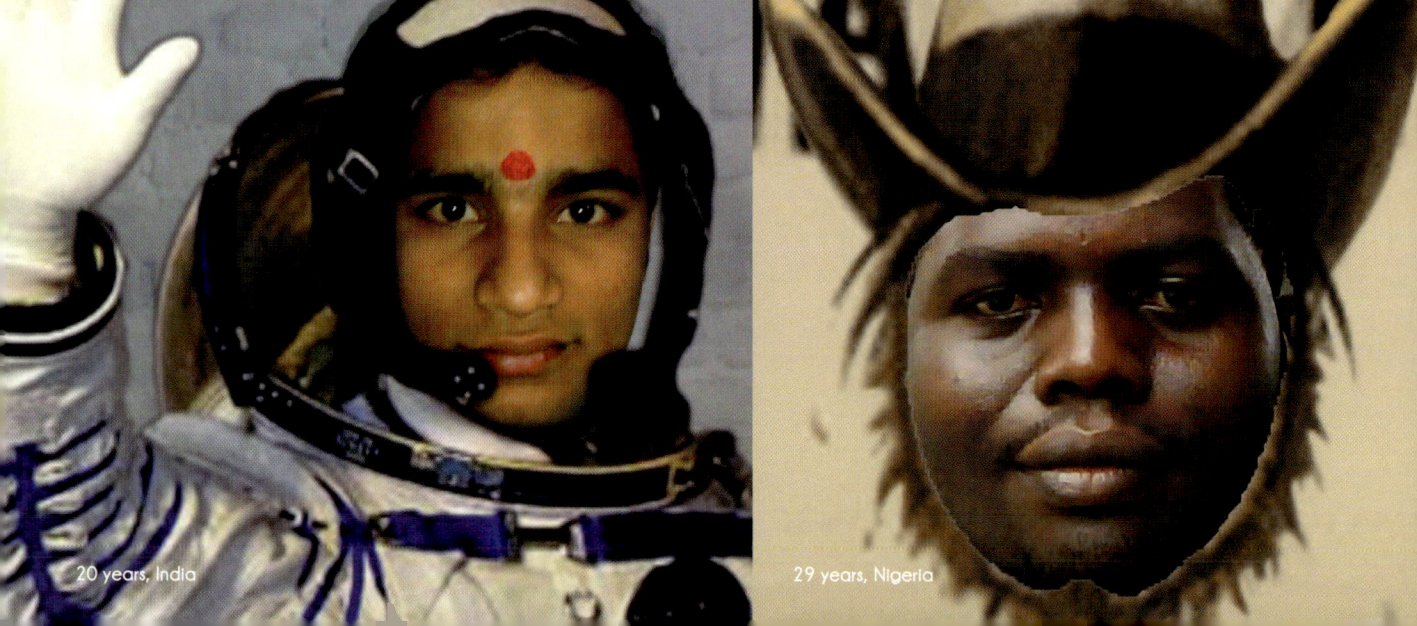

24 years, Nigeria

30 years, Indonesia

50 years, UK

30 years, Mexico

18 years, South Africa

20 years, India

29 years, Nigeria

32 years, Malaysia

29 years, Nigeria

38 years, UK

29 years, Sweden

26 years, Italy

PICTURE ENHANCEMENTS

29 years, Italy

Social-Network-Nutzer jeden Alters und aus allen Nationen haben aus dem Selbstporträt eine neue Kunstform entwickelt.

Mein Leben in Bildern. Für mich. Für meine Freunde. Für die ganze Welt.

Social network users of all ages and from all nations have developed a new form of art through self-portrait.

My life in pictures. For me. For my friends. For the whole world.

PEOPLE

BexyBoo   20 years, UK

Uploaded 02.06.10 10:27

PEOPLE - BexyBoo

Resolution: 960 x 1280 px

PEOPLE - BexyBoo

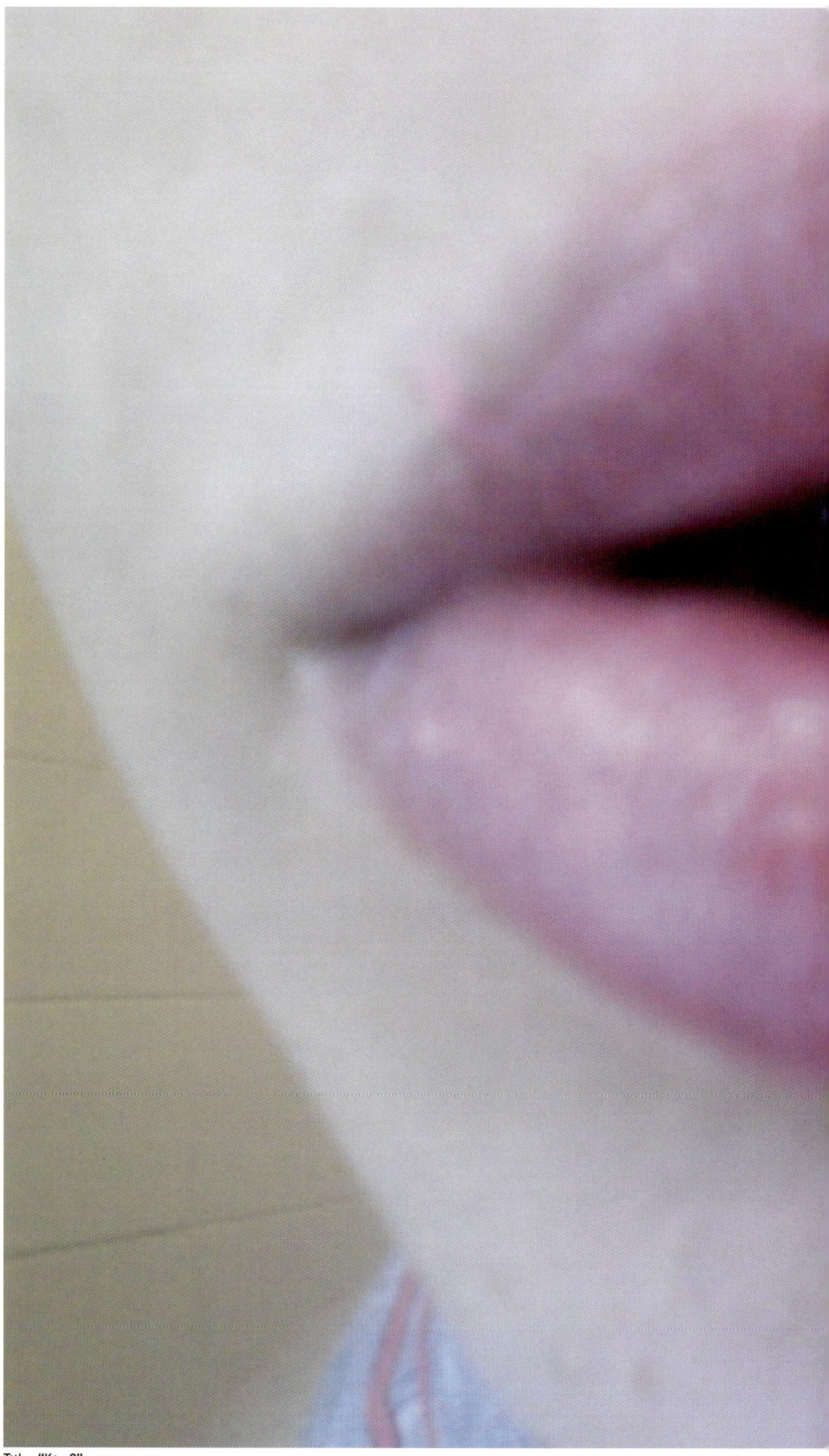

Title: "Kiss?"

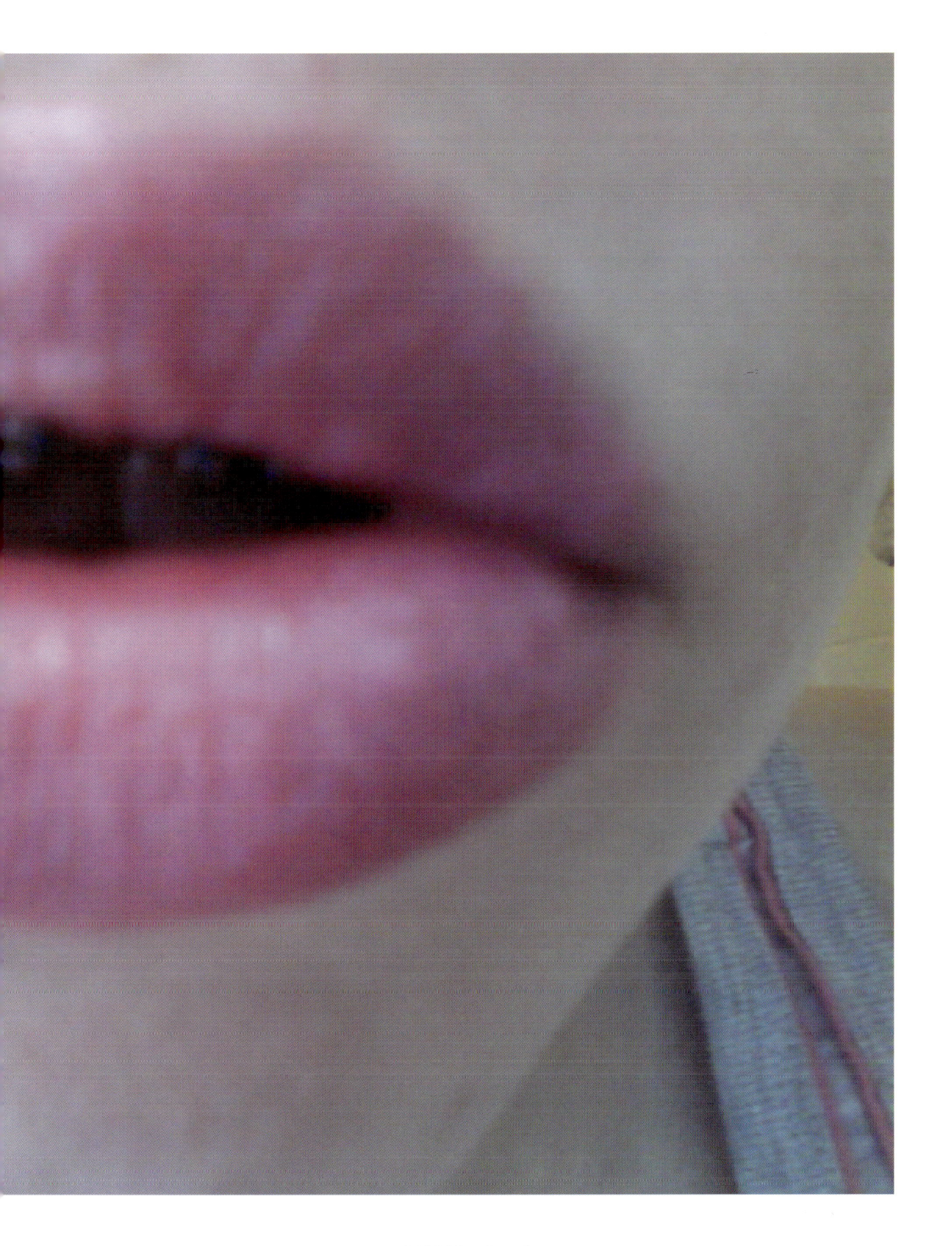

PEOPLE - BexyBoo

juggalette420   24 years, USA

Resolution: 480 x 640 px

PEOPLE - juggalette420

Resolution: 960 x 1280 px

Profile picture

Title: "My Vanz"

Title: "my tat. sad juggalette"

PEOPLE - juggalette420

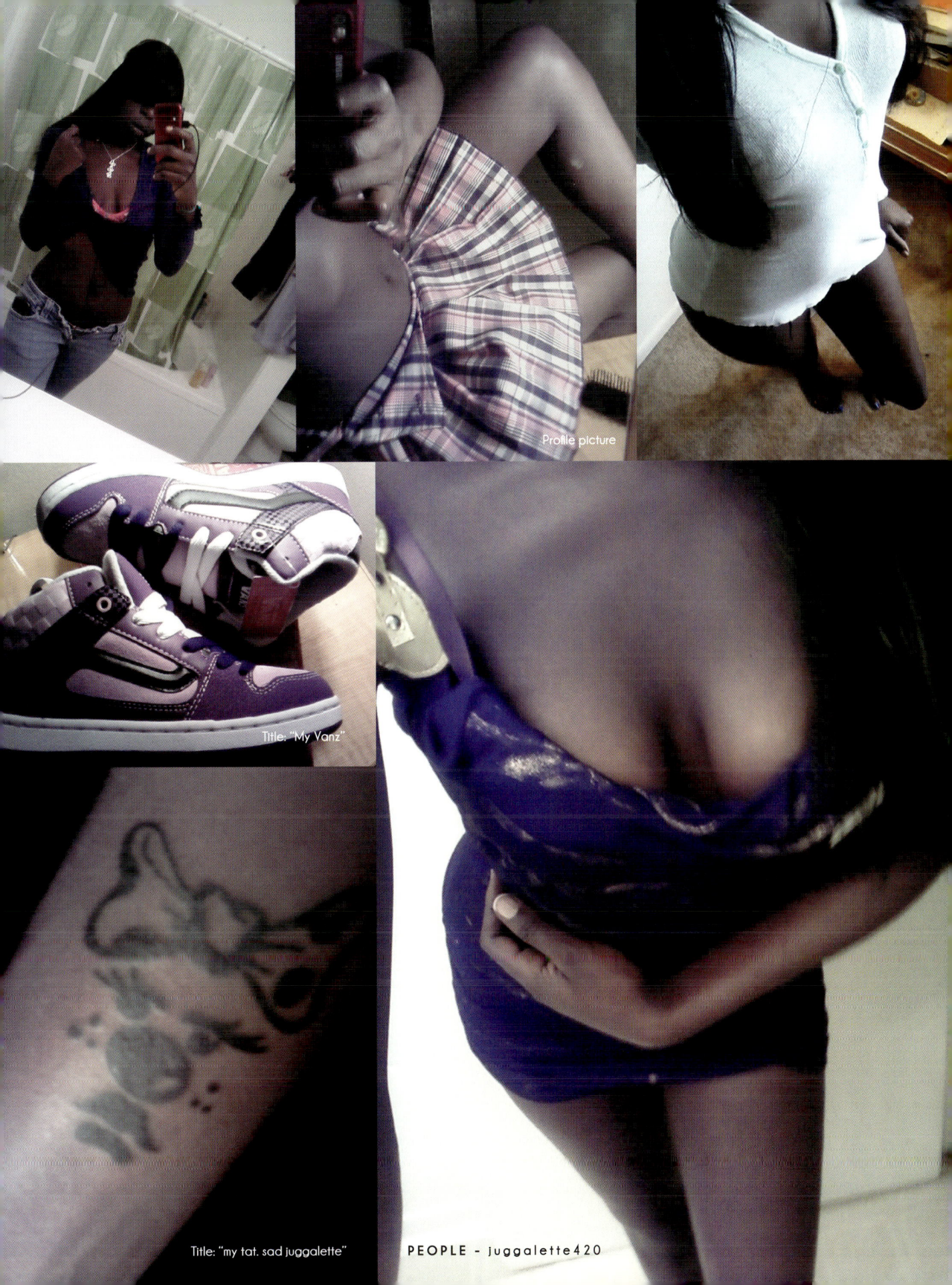

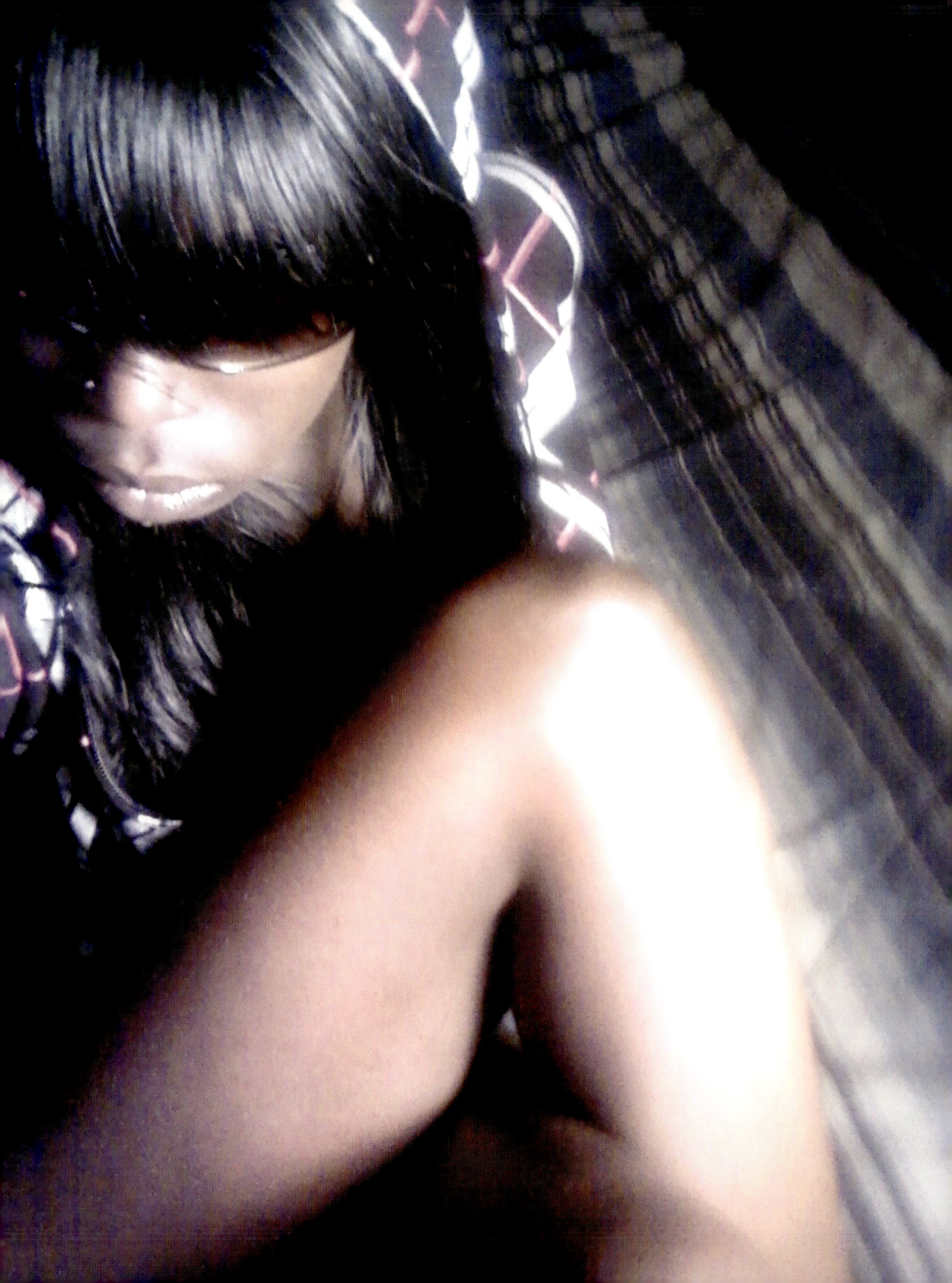

Uploaded 10.03.10 03:52

PEOPLE - juggalette420

suicide_em0 | 20 years, Philippines

Resolution all pictures: 240 x 320 px

PEOPLE - suicide_em0

Uploaded 09.03.09 12:54

Camera Nokia 6630

Uploaded 09.03.09 12:45

PEOPLE - suicide_em0

ladypr 27 years, Puerto Rico

Camera Samsung Propel™ Pro

PEOPLE - ladypr

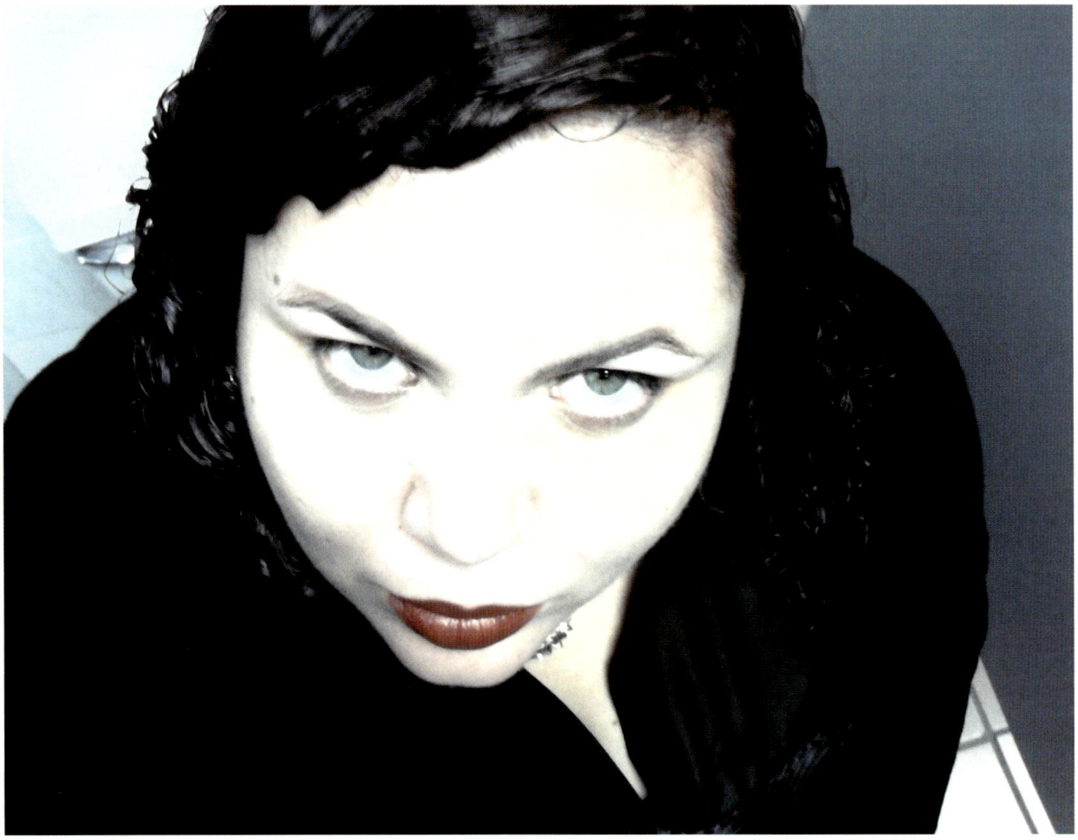

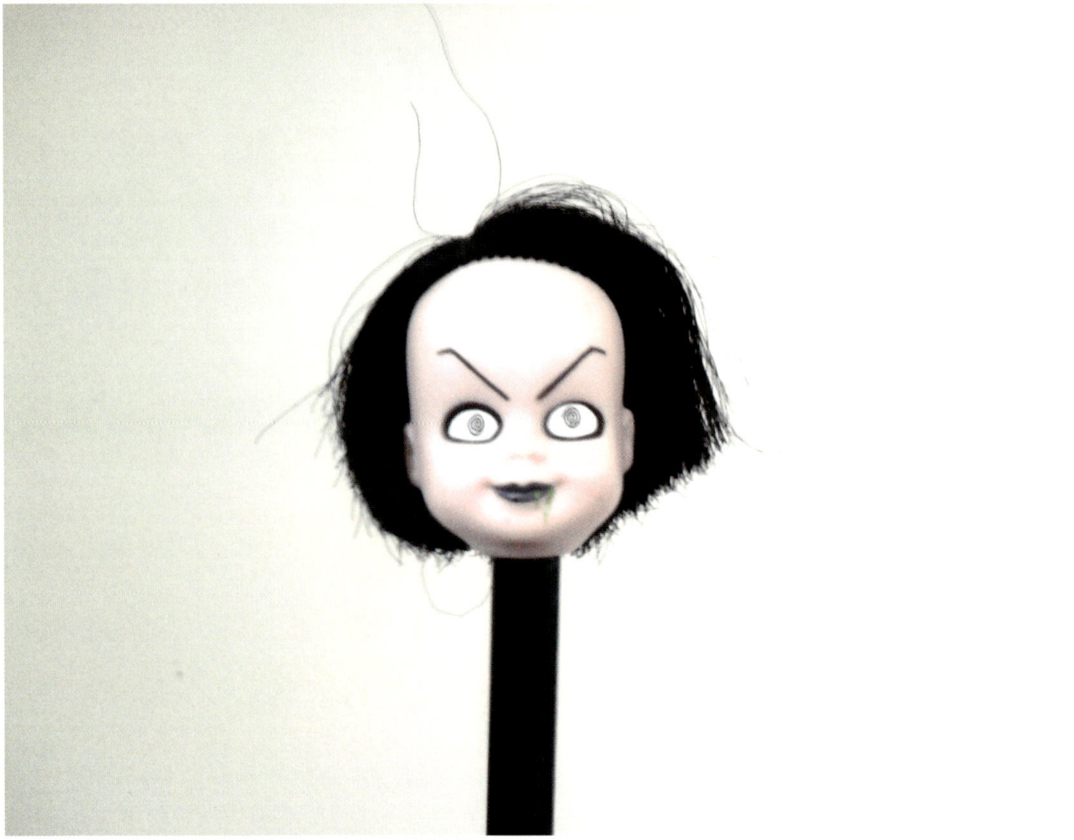

PEOPLE - ladypr

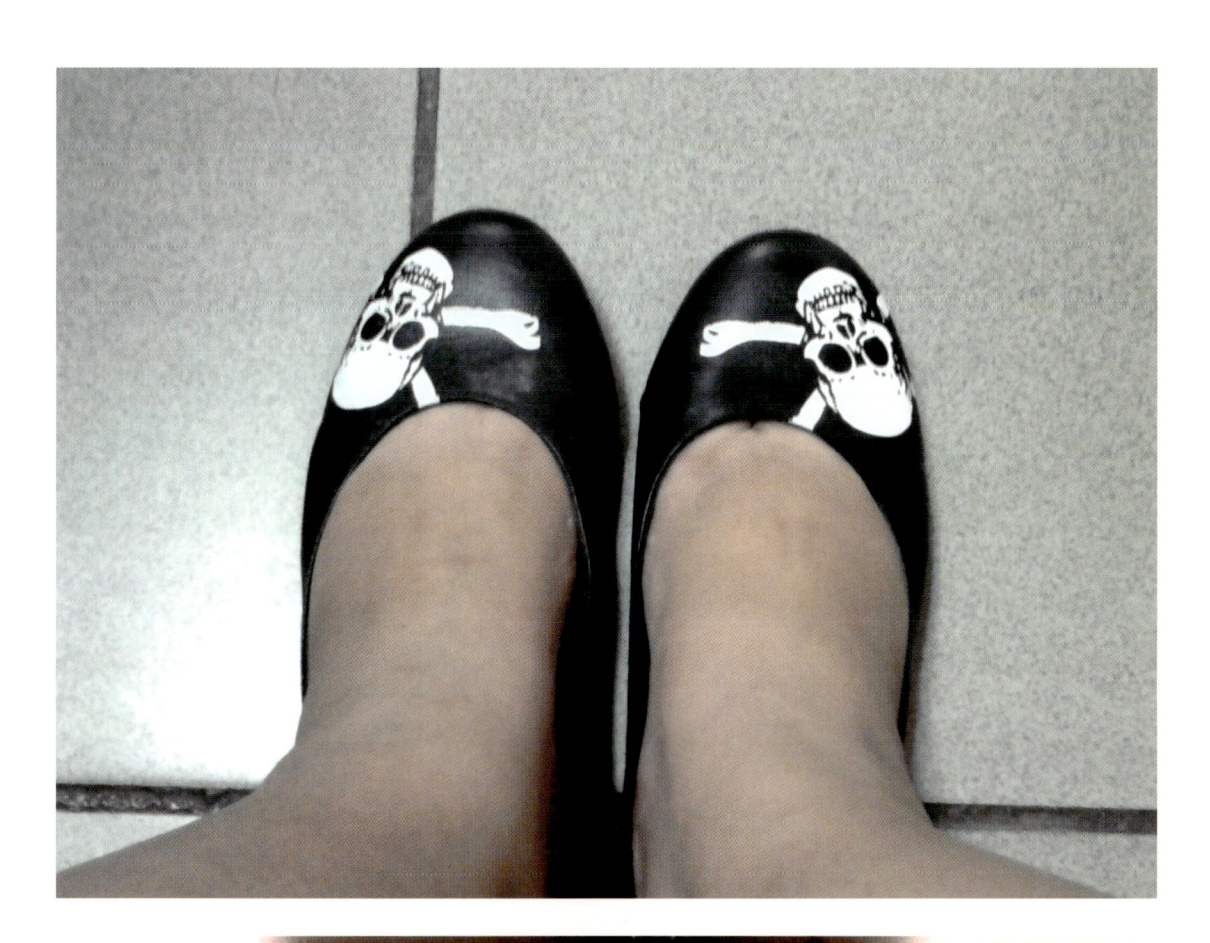

Resolution all pictures: 320 x 320 px

PEOPLE - ladypr

Resolution: 1600 x 1200

PEOPLE - ladypr

BaByBooB   25 years, Japan

Uploaded 24.07.10 04:04

PEOPLE - BaByBooB

Title: "My art nails"

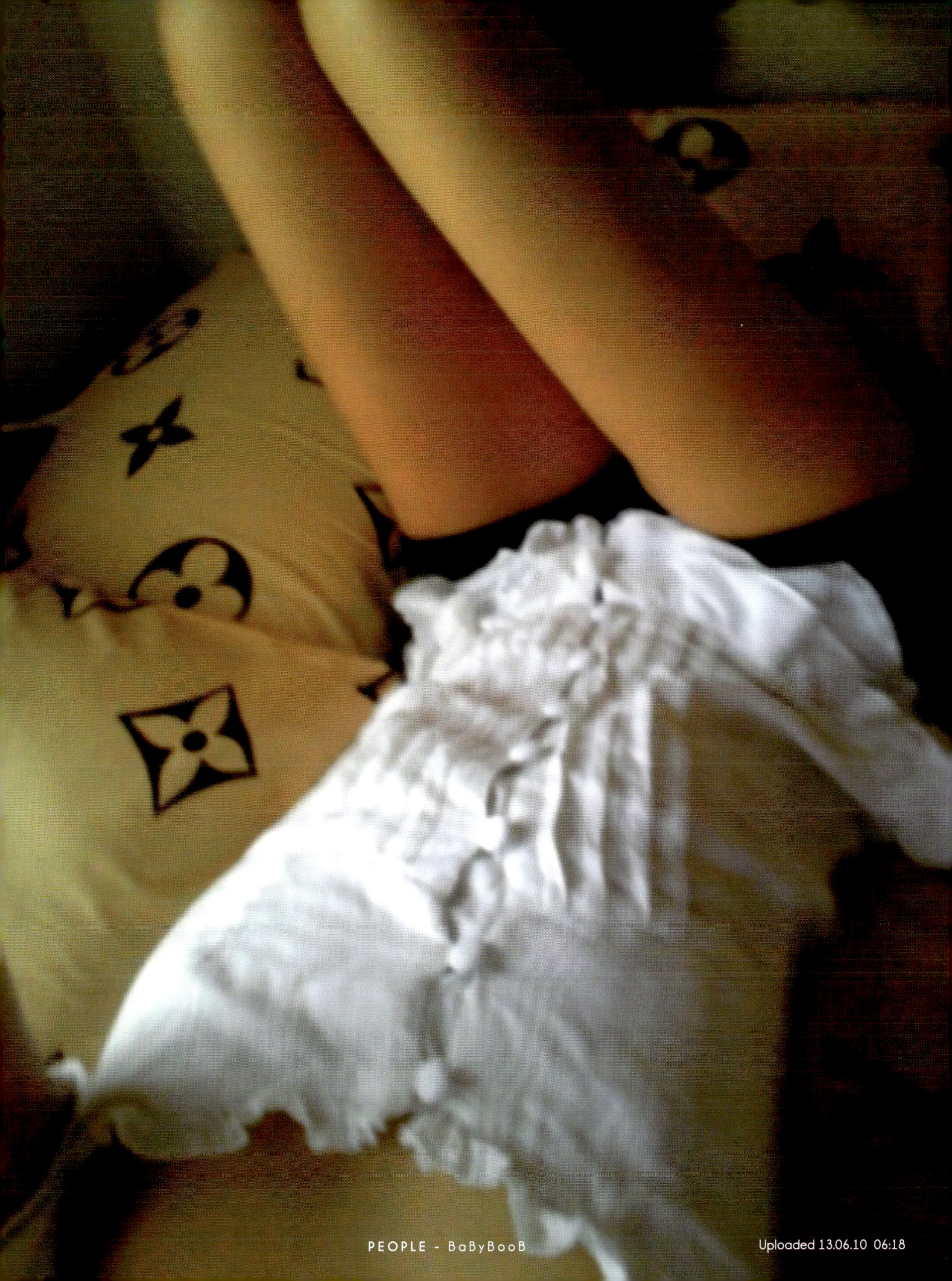

PEOPLE - BaByBooB Uploaded 13.06.10 06:18

Uploaded 13.07.10 20:33

PEOPLE - BaByBooB

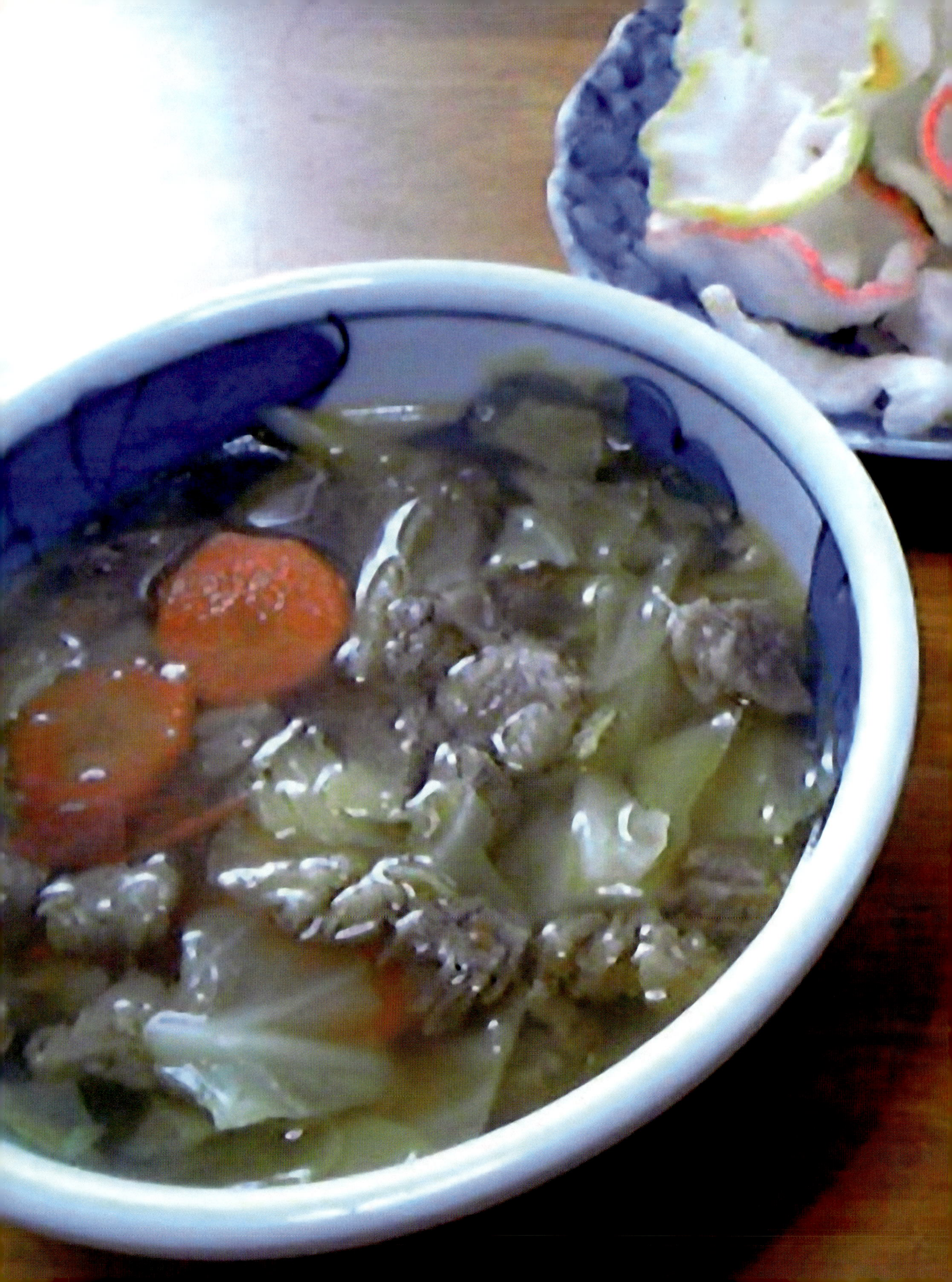

PEOPLE - BaByBooB

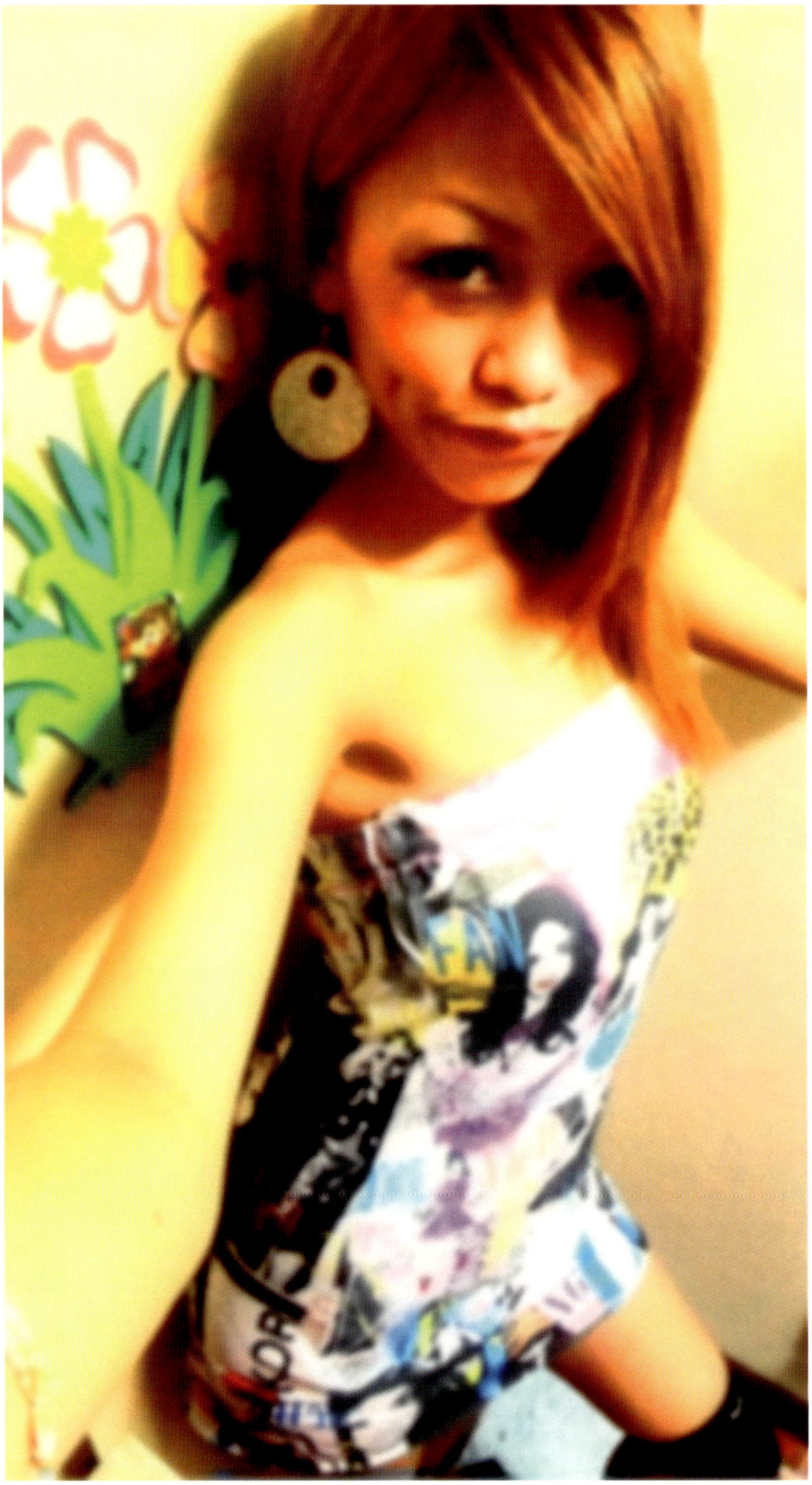

PEOPLE - BaByBooB

MIRvmn   29 years, Sweden

PEOPLE - MIRvmn

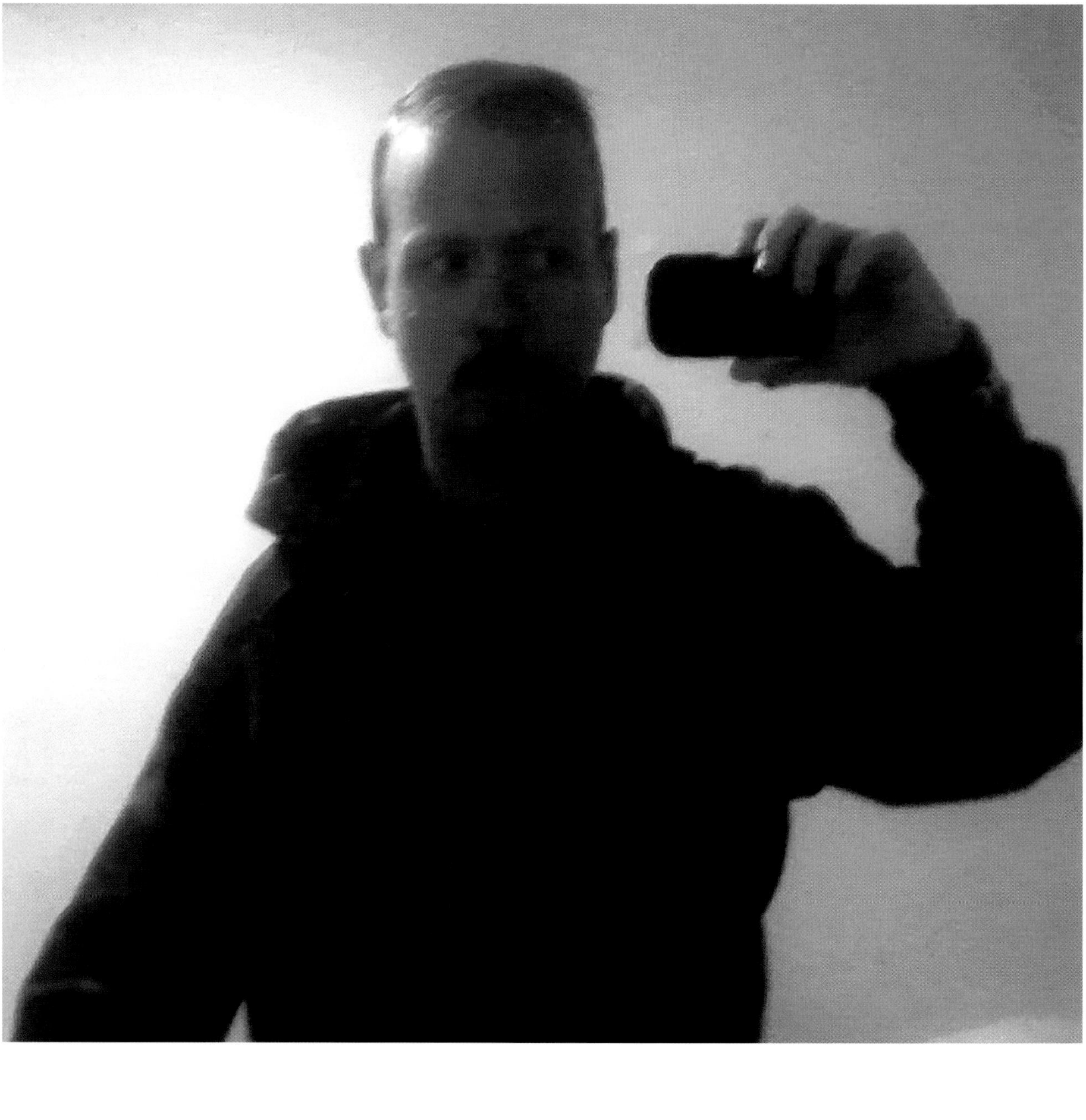

68 comments

PEOPLE - MlRvmn

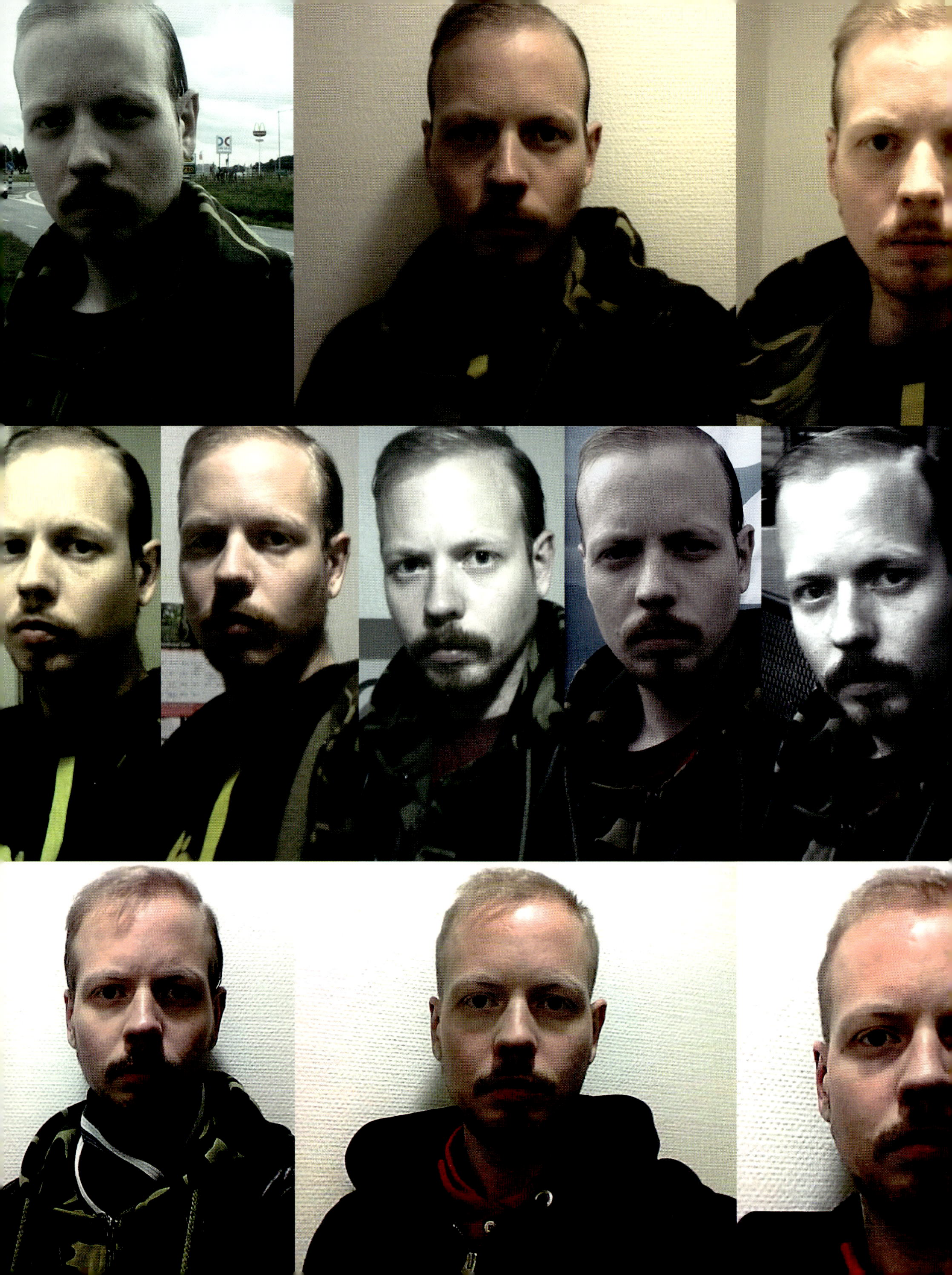

PEOPLE - MIRvmn

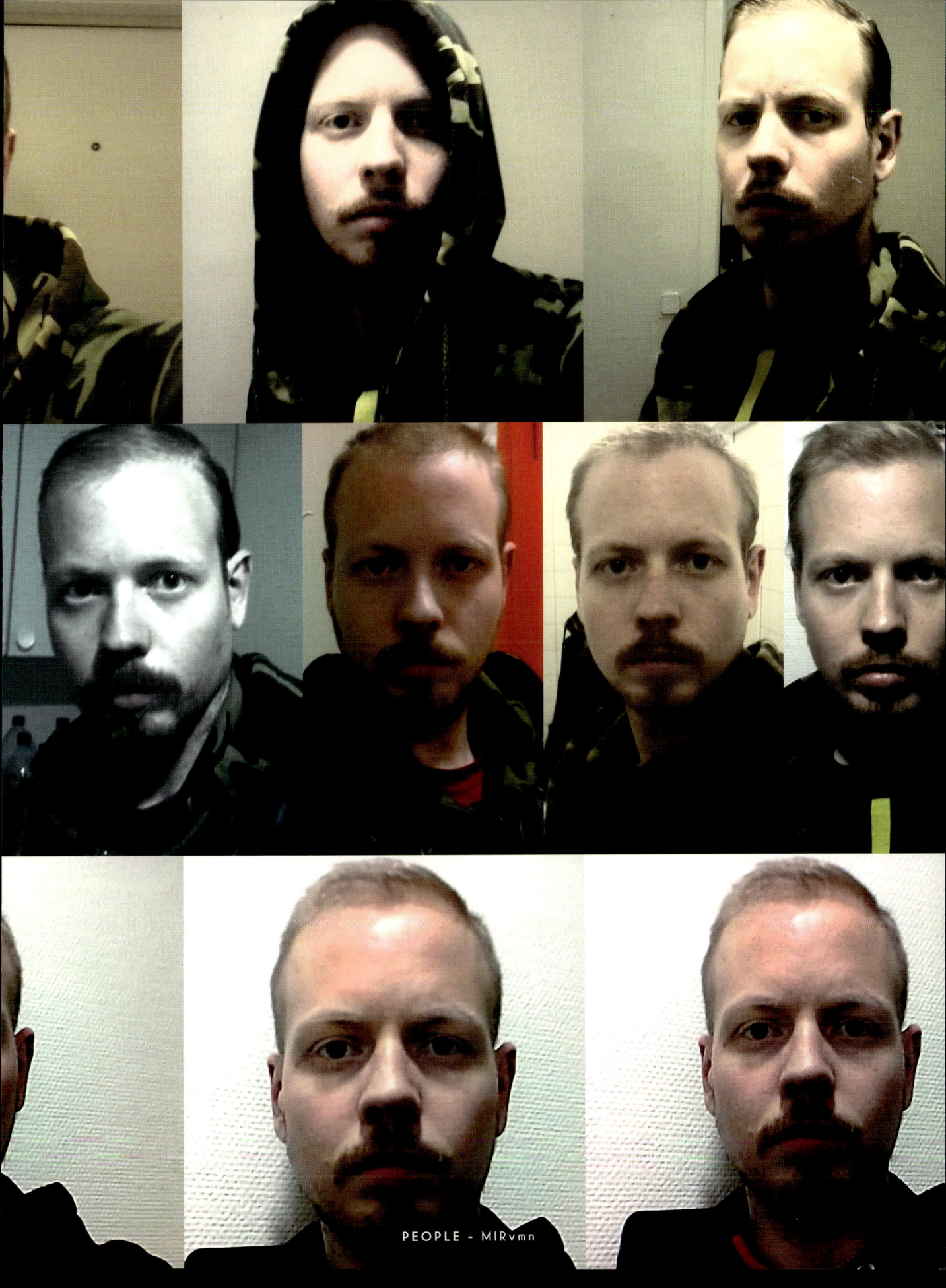

Natlove 26 years, USA

PEOPLE - Natlove

Title: "Ya la envidia no importa vota 0 sigo"

PEOPLE - Natlove

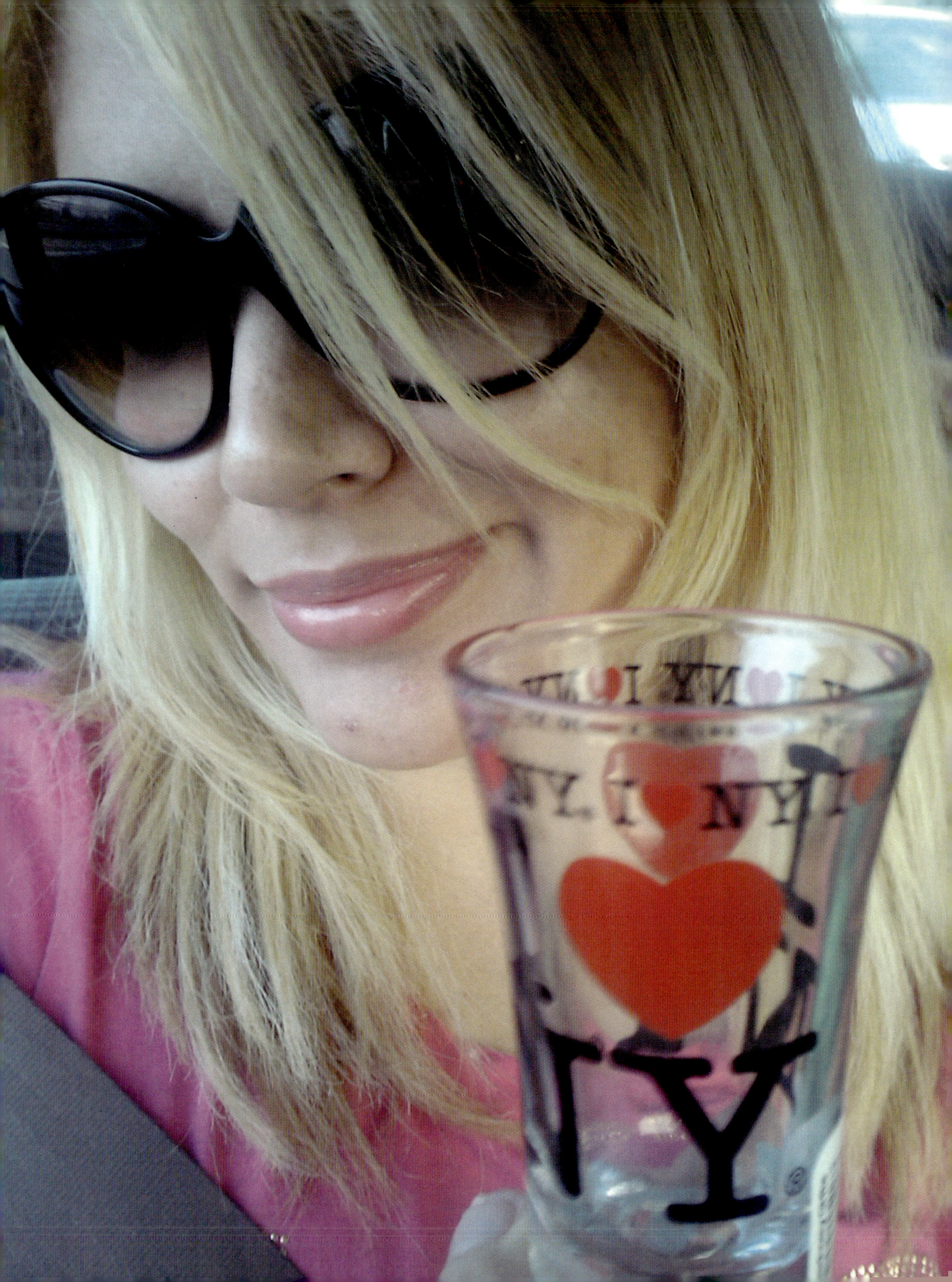

PEOPLE - Natlove

Title: "Da face of hangover"

PEOPLE - Natlove

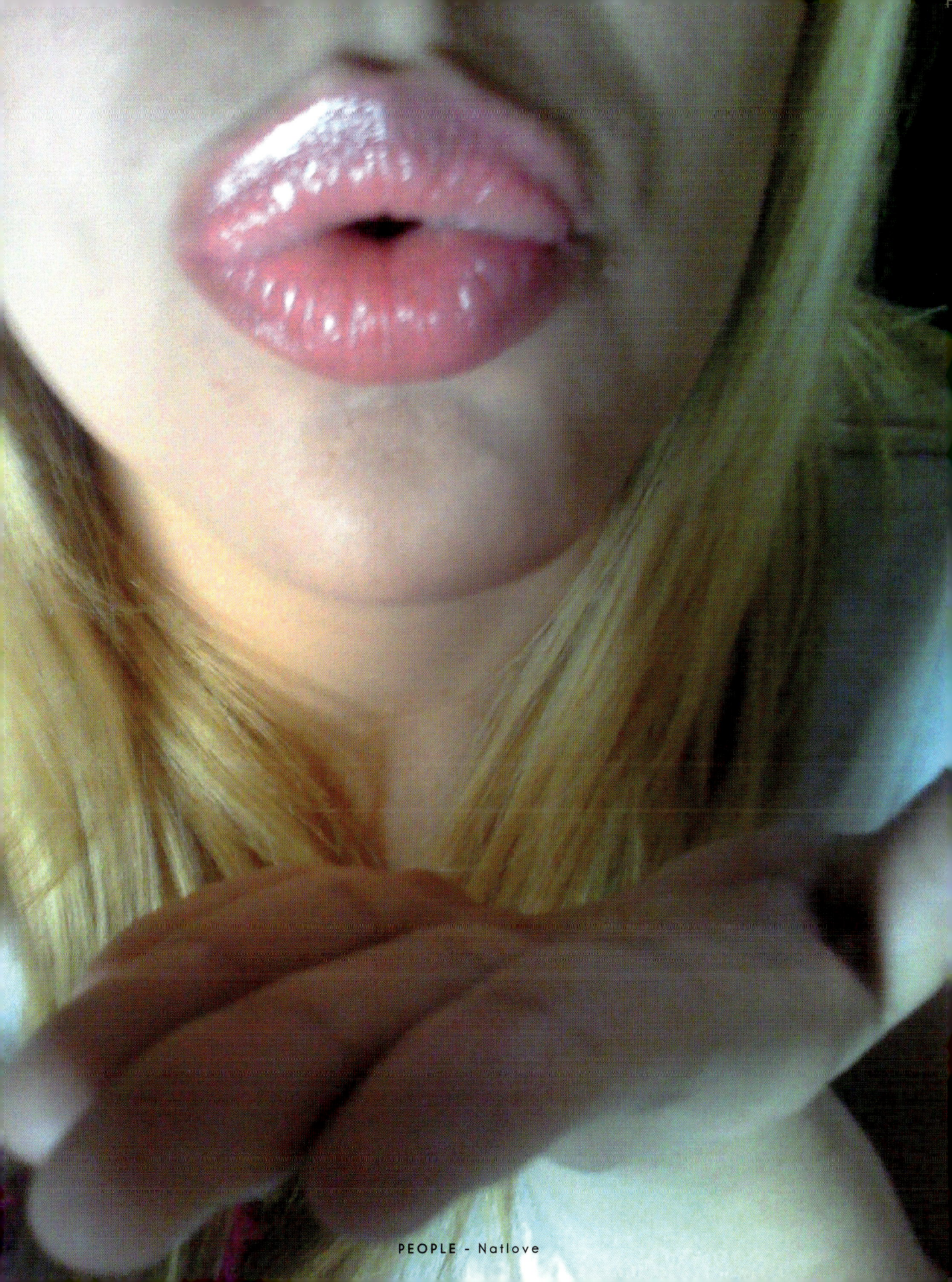

LoveASHIM | 33 years, India

Title: "Travelling"

PEOPLE - LoveASHIM

Uploaded 09.10.09 21:12

PEOPLE - LoveASHIM

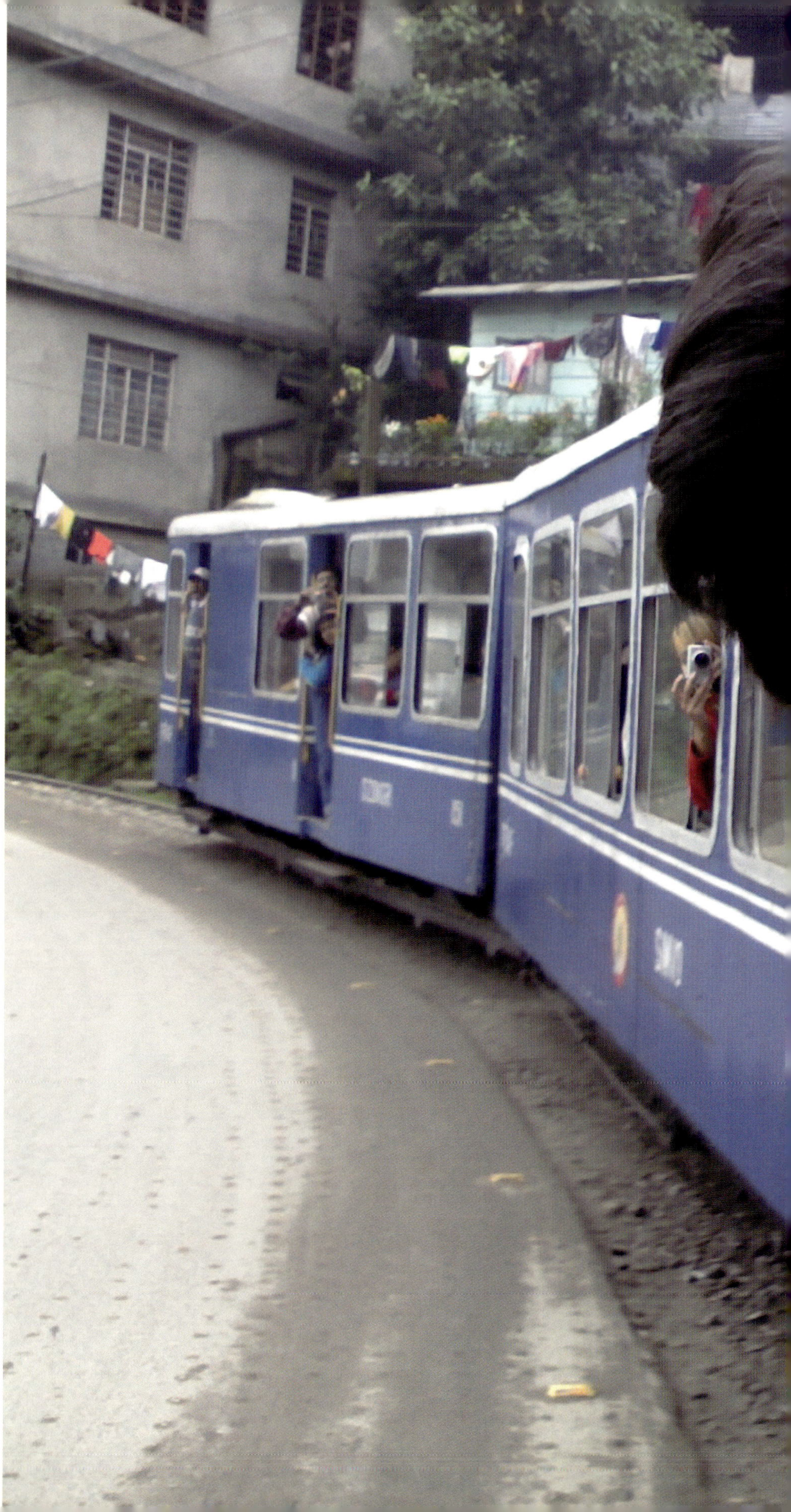

Uploaded 13.10.09 18:32

PEOPLE - LoveASHIM

Azumi4u 27 years, South Africa

PEOPLE - Azumi4u

Camera Samsung U900 Soul

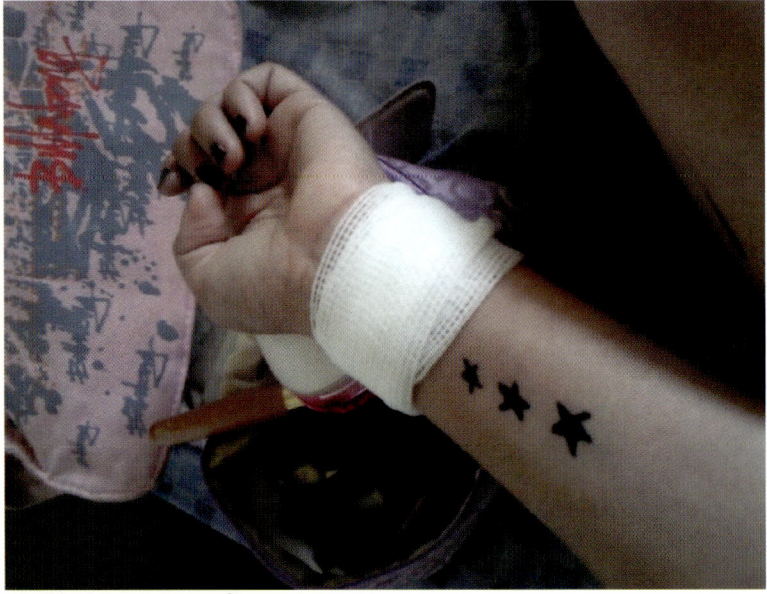

Title: "Got hurt . . . . Auuuuu :("

Title: "Thick around d waist pretty in d face"

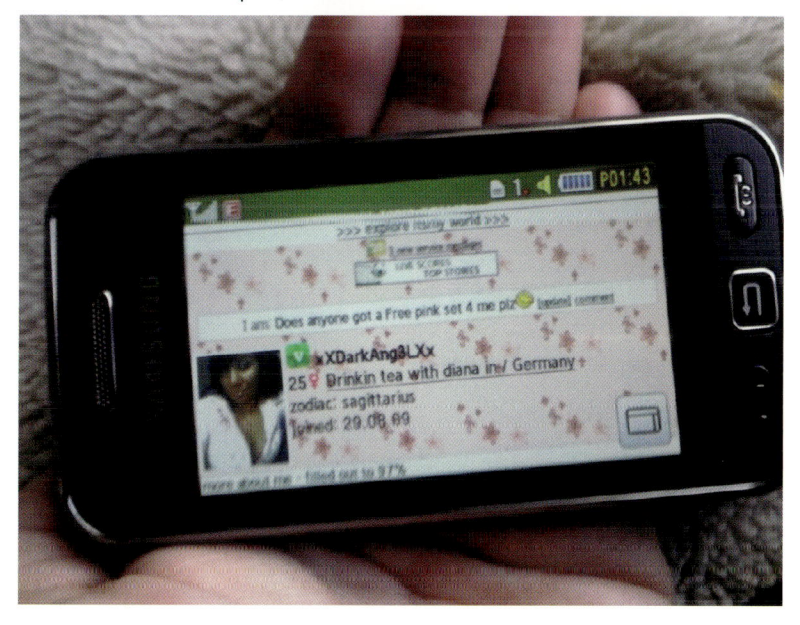

PEOPLE - Azumi4u

Title: "Lovin this shoe.."

PEOPLE - Azumi4u

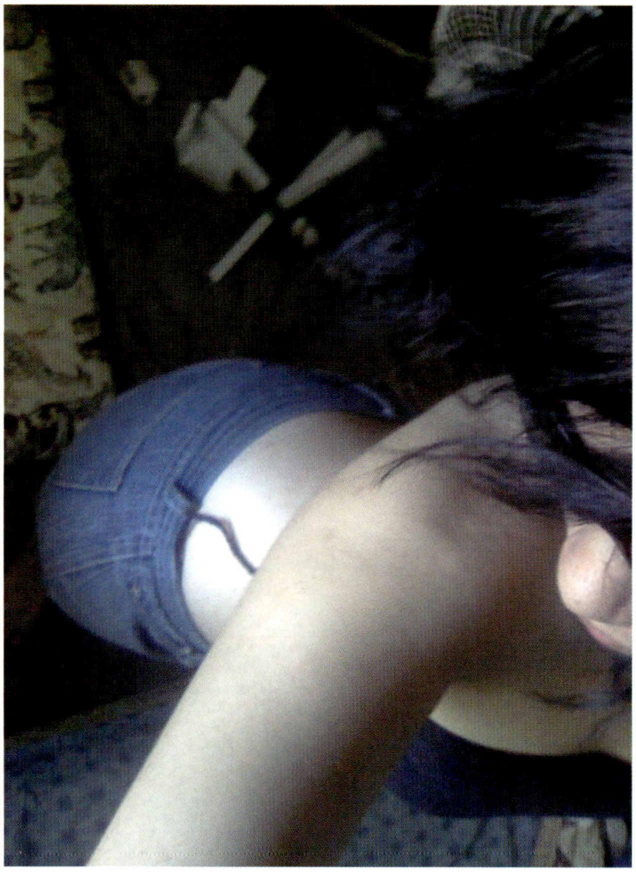 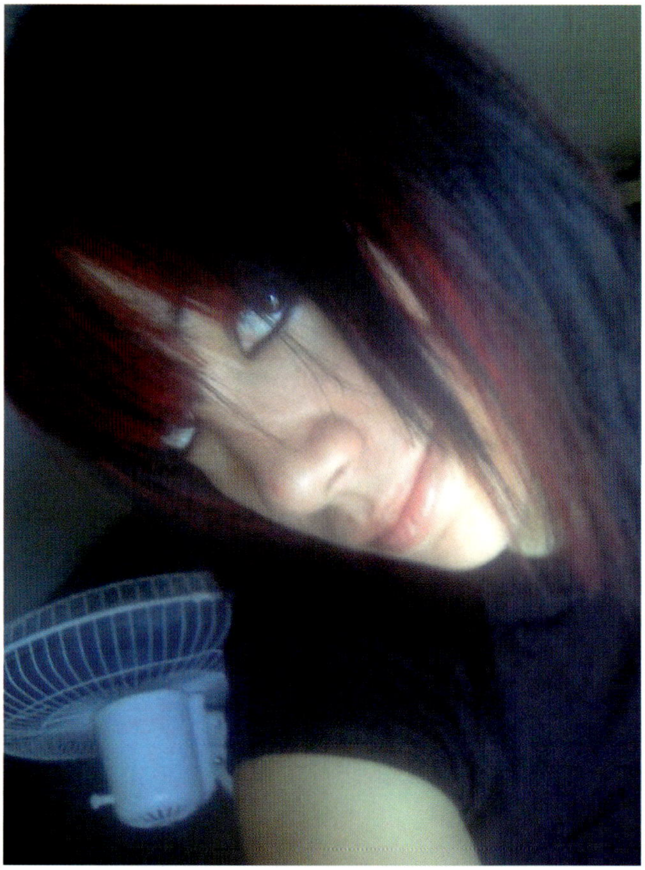

PEOPLE - Azumi4u

Rose4u1986   24 years, India

PEOPLE - Rose4u1986

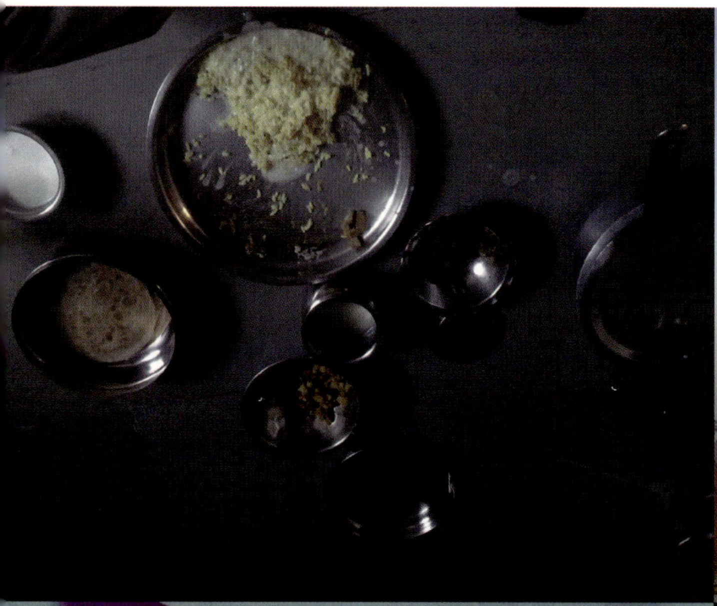
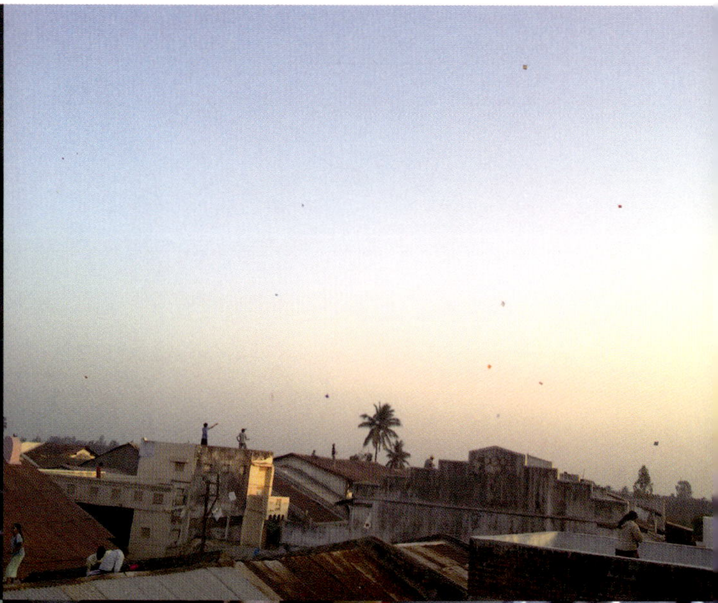
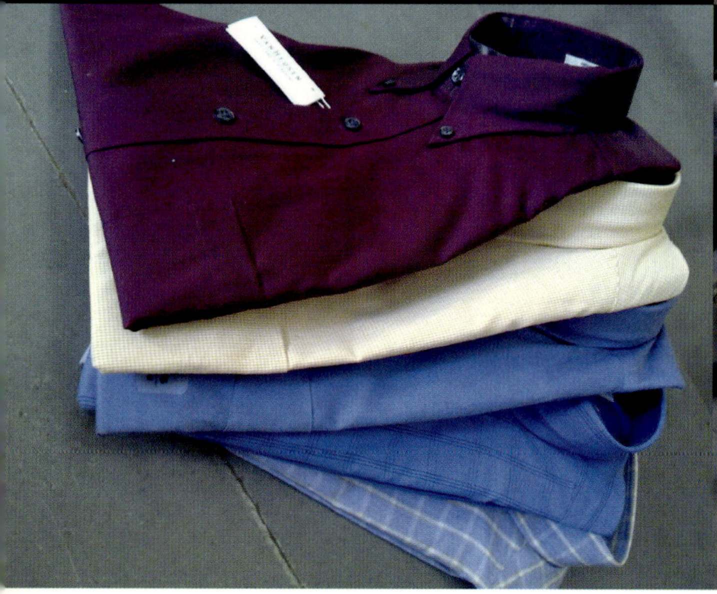
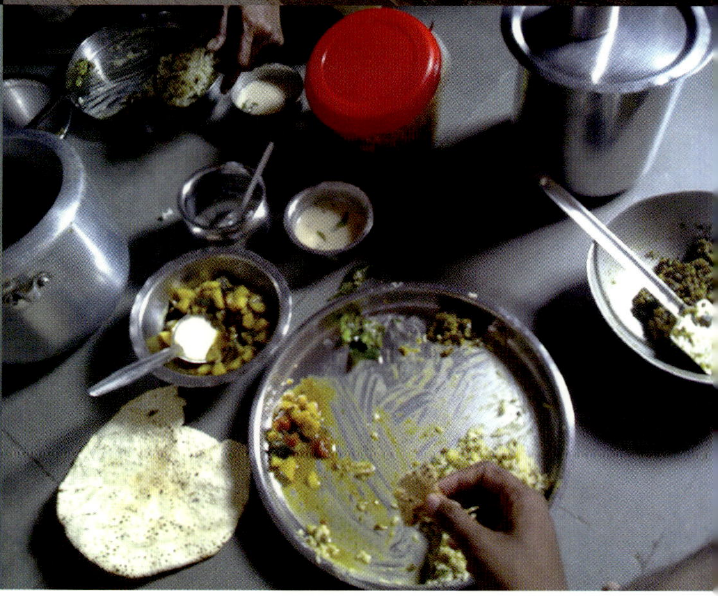

Title: "My dinner"

PEOPLE - Rose4u1986

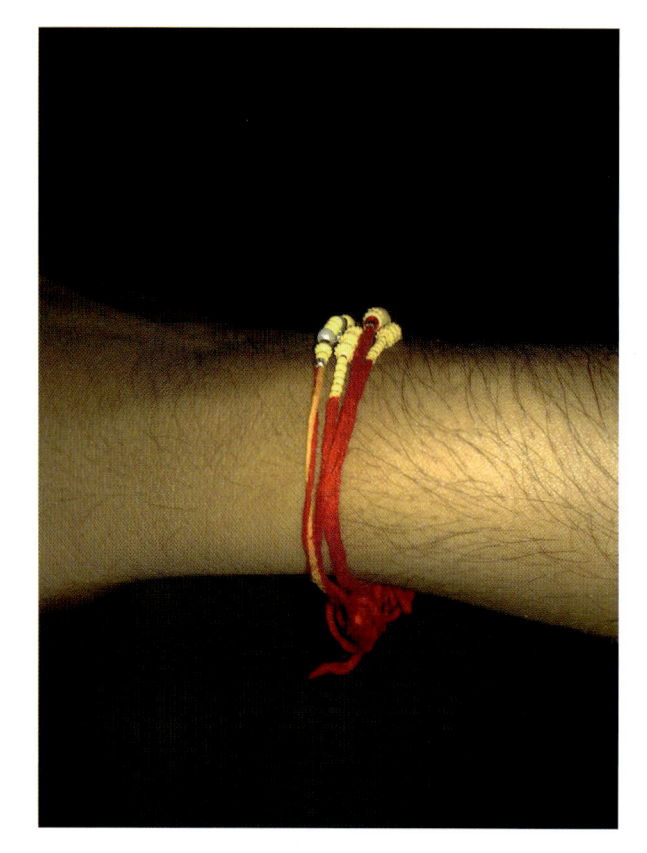

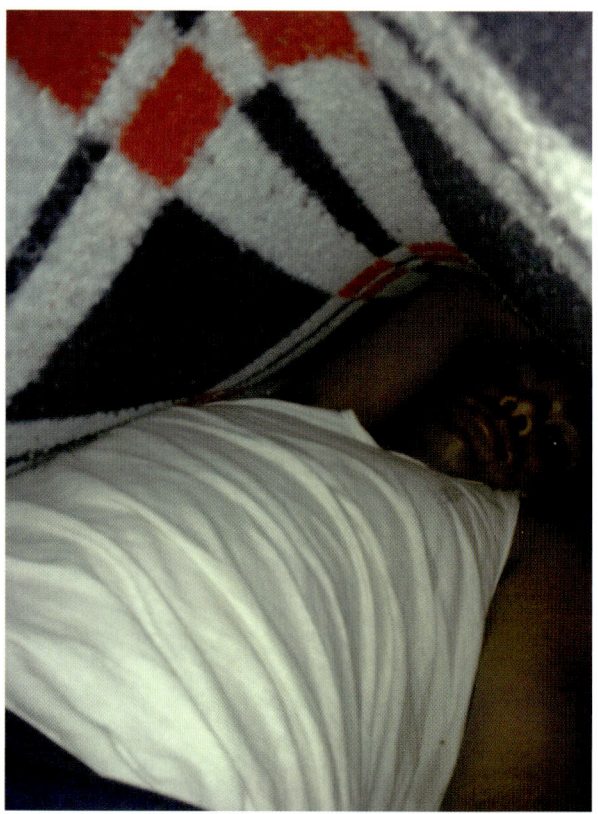

Title: "early morning under blanket..doing chat"

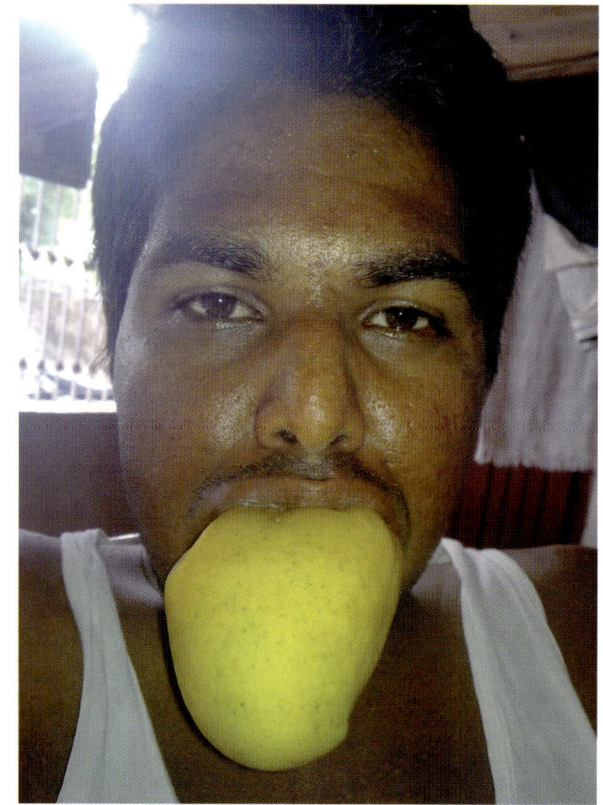

Camera Nokia N79

PEOPLE - Rose4u1986

_-_ALeSaNa_-_ 21 years, Argentina

Camera Nokia 5310 Xpressmusic

PEOPLE - _-_ALeSaNa_-_

Profile picture

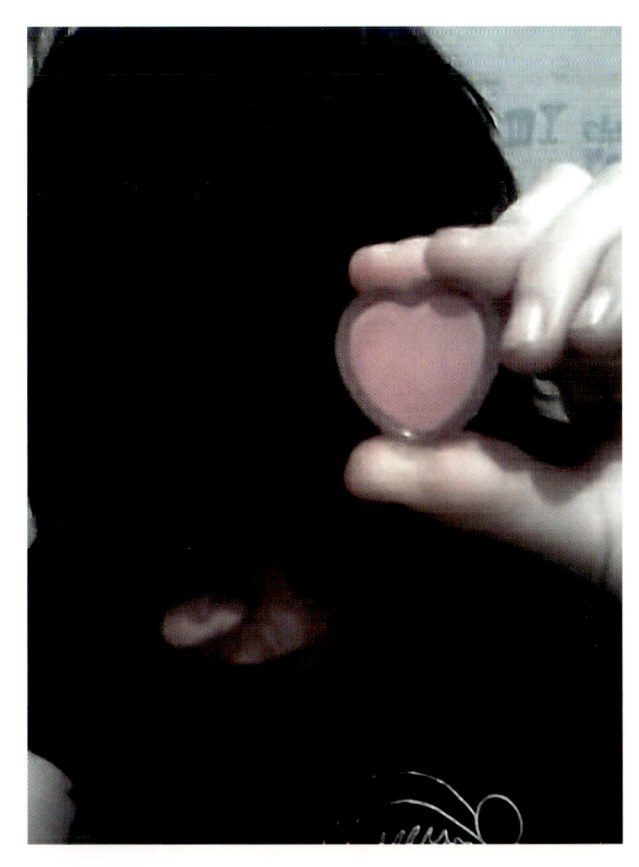

PEOPLE - _-_ALeSaNa_-_

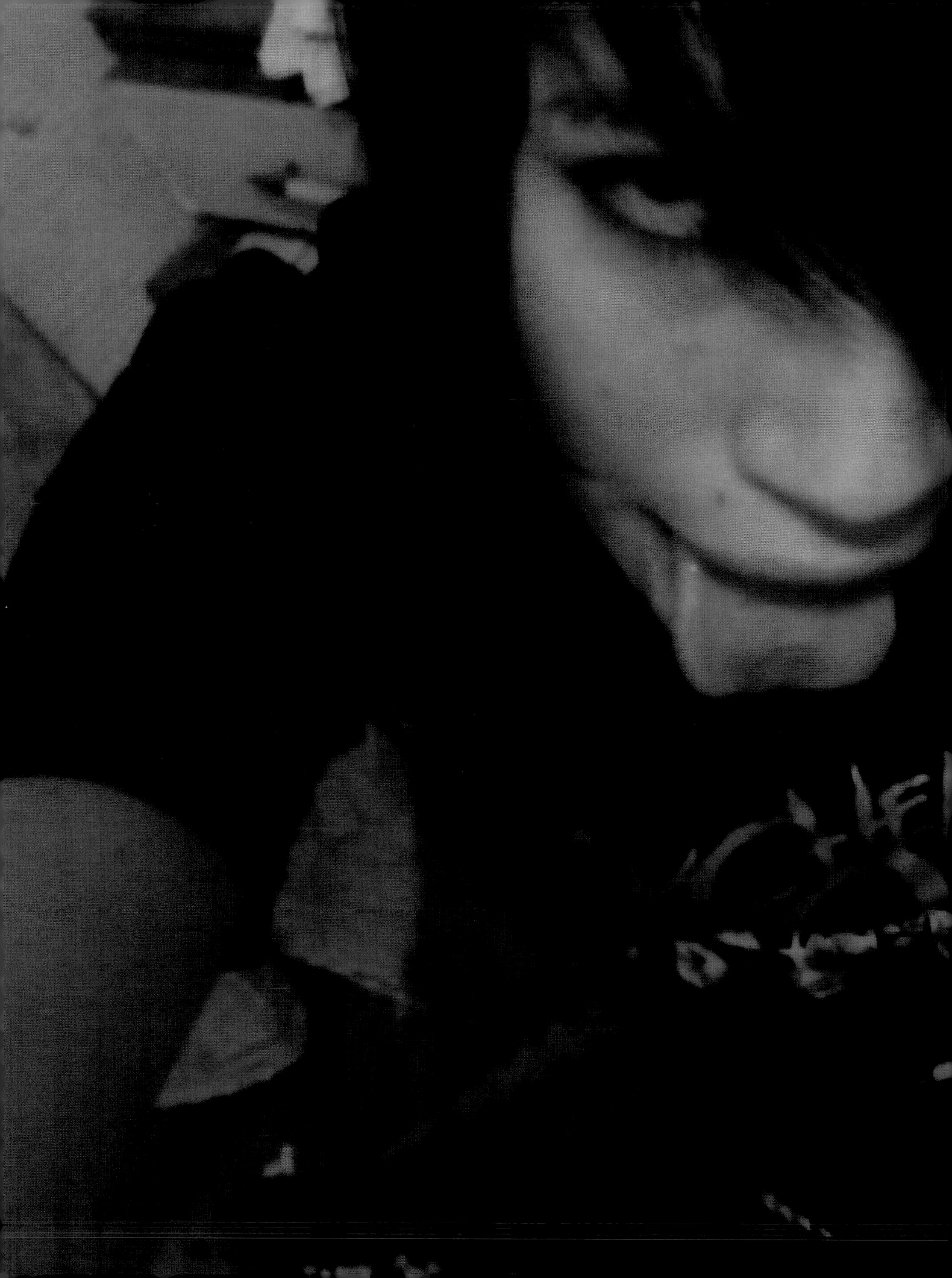

PEOPLE - _-_ALeSaNa_-_

Xivir   20 years, Guatemala

PEOPLE - XIvir

ESJ LET IT LOVE U

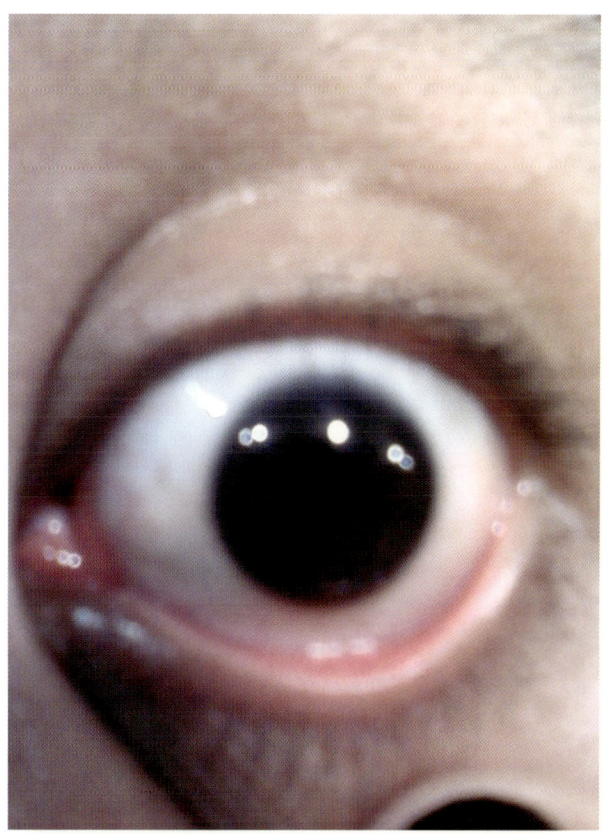

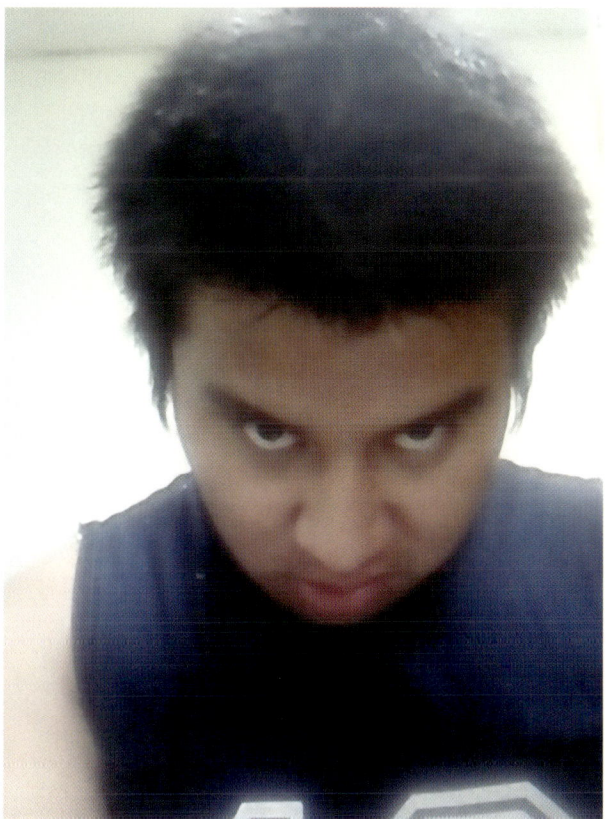

PEOPLE - XIvIr

Camera Samsung Messager™

PEOPLE - XIvir

FACTS

65% der weltweiten Social-Network-Nutzer kommunizieren in mehr als einer Sprache. In Deutschland und Italien sprechen fast **75%** eine zweite Sprache.

8% der weltweiten Social-Network-Nutzer mögen den Frühling, weil ihre Freundinnen sich dann nicht mehr über das schlechte Wetter beschweren. **21%** der deutschen Social-Network-Nutzer mögen den Frühling, weil sie ihr Mobiltelefon dann wieder benutzen können, ohne sich die Finger zu erfrieren.

Dies ist die Weihnachtswunschliste der weltweiten Social-Network-Nutzer: **1.** Geld **2.** Ein neues Mobiltelefon. **3.** Neue Kleidung. In Nigeria und Indien ist ein neues Mobiltelefon nicht unter den **Top 3**, sondern es sind Urlaubsreisen, Unterstützung im Haushalt/beim Lernen und neue Kleidung.

Die beliebtesten Sommer-Erfrischungsgetränke weltweit: **29%** Softdrinks mit viel Eis, **21%** Eistee. In Spanien ziehen **31%** Eiskaffee vor, **23%** Eistee.

In Südafrika und Großbritannien haben mehr als **70%** der Social-Network-Nutzer keine Kamera mehr, sondern machen all ihre Fotos mit dem Handy.

64% der Social-Network-Nutzer tauschen ihr Profilbild aus, sobald sie ein neues, cooles Selbstporträt gemacht haben. **5%** geben an, dass sie überhaupt kein Profilbild haben.

38% der Iren nehmen das erste Selbstporträt, das sie machen, als neues Profilbild. **70%** der Italiener machen zehn oder mehr Bilder von sich, bevor sie eines für ihr Profil wählen, nur **15%** veröffentlichen ihren ersten Versuch.

30% der weltweiten Nutzer haben schon einmal ein Profilbild gelöscht, weil es negative Kommentare oder Votes bekommen hat.

•Alle Zahlen aus Nutzerumfragen auf m.itsmy.com

65% of social network users worldwide communicate in more than one language.
In Germany and Italy, almost **75%** of users speak at least one other language.

8% of social network users worldwide look forward to spring because it means their girlfriends will stop complaining about the cold weather. **21%** of German social network users like spring because they can type and chat on their mobile phones without frozen fingers.

The Christmas wish list of social network users worldwide: **1.** Money. **2.** A new mobile phone. **3.** New clothes. In Nigeria and India a new mobile phone doesn't feature in the **Top 3,** but rather holiday trips, household/learning support and new clothes.

Favourite summer refreshments worldwide: **29%** of users prefer soft drinks with a lot of ice, **21%** prefer ice tea. In Spain, **31%** of users prefer ice coffee, **23%** prefer ice tea.

In South Africa and Great Britain, more than **70%** of social network users no longer own a camera, but take all their photos with their mobile phone.

64% of social network users change their profile picture whenever they have a new, cool self-portrait. **5%** don't have a profile picture at all.

38% of Irish people use the first self-portrait they take as their new profile picture. **70%** of Italians take at least ten pictures of themselves before they choose one for their profile; only **15%** publish their first attempt.

30% of users worldwide have deleted a profile picture due to negative comments or votes.

•All figures taken from user surveys created at m.itsmy.com

ABOUT THE EDITORS

LAURA PIANTONI

Die Künstlerin Laura Piantoni (geboren 1977) arbeitet vor allem in den Bereichen Fotografie und Siebdruck, die sie an der Münchner Kunstakademie (1999–2006) und an der Hochschule für Gestaltung und Kunst Zürich (2001) studierte. Insbesondere interessiert sie sich für die Darstellung des Menschen in inszenierten Porträts und in zu Künstlerbüchern zusammengefassten Momentaufnahmen ihres näheren Umfelds. Piantoni gewann mehrere Fotopreise und ihre Arbeiten werden international in zahlreichen Einzel- und Gruppenausstellungen gezeigt. Ihr aktueller Arbeitsschwerpunkt ist Social Art, inspiriert von der Fotografie sozialer Netzwerke.

Laura Piantoni (born 1977) is a Munich-based artist focusing primarily on photography and silkscreen printing. She concentrated on these areas whilst studying at the Academy of Fine Arts Munich, Germany, (1999–2006) and the Zurich University of the Arts, Switzerland, (2001). She is particularly interested in human portrayal, both staged portraits as well as snapshotlike photographs of her surroundings, and combining them into artists' books. The winner of numerous photography prizes, Piantoni has organised and participated in several solo and group shows throughout the world. Her current focus is on social art, which is inspired by social network photography.

SABINE IRRGANG

Sabine Irrgang (geboren 1966) ist COO und Mitgründerin der Gofresh GmbH, München, Deutschland. Sie ist seit 2001 im Mobile Business tätig und wurde vom Mobile Entertainment Magazine in den Jahren 2008, 2009 und 2010 als eine der Top-50-Frauen im Mobile-Content-Business weltweit gelistet. Sabine Irrgang ist ein Gesicht der Kampagne zur IHK-Wahl 2011 (für München und Oberbayern) und Mitglied des Dell Women's Entrepreneur Network (DWEN).

Sabine Irrgang (born 1966) is COO and Co-Founder of Gofresh GmbH, Munich, Germany. She has been in mobile business since 2001, and was listed as one of the Top 50 Women in the mobile content business worldwide by Mobile Entertainment Magazine in 2008, 2009 and 2010. Sabine Irrgang is a face of the campaign for the Chamber of Commerce's 2011 election (Munich and Upper Bavaria) and a member of the Dell Women's Entrepreneur Network (DWEN).

ACKNOWLEDGEMENTS

Wir danken all unseren Freunden weltweit für das tolle Material, die großartigen Fotos, die sie uns zur Verfügung gestellt haben, und dafür, dass sie uns das Recht zum Abdruck ihrer Fotos erteilt haben:

We would like to thank all our friends around the world for the brilliant material, the amazing photos they provided us with, and for granting us the right to print their photos:

-_ALeSaNa_-, _JULIETA_, 2010females, 52-Blackbird, Aakash24, angel_d_tenebre, An-Nissa, annroscoo, AsHaLeE, Assfy, auraku, Axes1854, Ayazone, Azumi4u, BaByBooB, Be333, bEbE_pReCioSa, Beckeiigh-boobz, Beverley2, BexyBoo, Blacktear, Blondeegirl, Boju01, Charles4al, Collycj, Curtis-09, DEEP-KUL-DEEP, diana-matiz, donlaurent, ELFADER1, Elisha1, eliza29, Em23mansfield, Franmerida, Funky-bee, Giambaru2, great_basil001, H0T-MALE, HANDSOME, Heavensend, Highney, hottiegirl4u, iced_heartX, Indie1, Ippyshakes, itsmemark123, Jacky_Rose, Jaidenlee, jarot, Jeopody, jeromxy, Joanne26, Jojo72, Joker68, jshock007, juggalette420, k_flex, Kaibil01, Kaz26, Kim0ya, krime, lady_vee, ladypr, Leo114930586, loubylou, LoveASHIM, Luvinit5, LvYOUlongTIME, Magda2592, Magicman99, Mandiemay, MaR1aNa_7, mdulayza, MeSuez, mikko, MIRvmn, MizzBrunette, montana, Mrhottest, Mudi-k, Muyis, nachos, nahF_mayte, Nasky2, Native1, Natlove, neoza-box, Netwa, NewEra, Neylla, Notty_BoY, Ntando25, NYCITYGUY, One-Luv, OnweIsreal, p0is0n_h0n3y, Parranderoboy, perfect-amigo, Pertual, Pinki, PRELICIOUS, prince247, Prince-nuel1000, Prostolos, puschi, rajanik, Revivence, Riniz, Rociolatina, Rockid, Rose4u1986, sameersahay, Sdumz, Seanify, SenatorD, sexyJD, sky-watcher, SLIM81, suicide_em0, Swagg_BreakA101, Tagz-3, Terrible84, ThatOneGirl_0x, TheRoad, Tju-tju, Unikat, Vampirin, venkatgece87, Vikasmagic, vince, Viuda, Waaj1, Westlaw, Wieny, Xivir, xXDarkAng3LXx_, Yesicas, ZaDiikA, ZedBe

Außerdem bedanken wir uns bei

We would also like to thank

Maria Ißl, Toni Montana Werner, Jukka Saarelainen, Mikko Saarelainen, Matthias Hein, Diana Taut Aslau, David SAID Mayerhofer

sowie

as well as

Michael Hutterer, Thorsten Wohlfarth, Matthias Wiegele, Sven For, Moni Neise, Katharina Korrek, Ajit Jaokar, Gary Kibel, Steve Glas, Sarah Schäfer, Mona Kassai, Tobias Weise, Jutta Friedrich, Rebecca Radovanovic, Karin Hofkirchner-Weigand, Inge Irrgang, Willi Mayerhofer, Albert Piantoni

Ganz besonders bedanken wir uns bei
ANTONIO VINCE STAYBL

Last but by no means least, a huge thank you to

IMPRINT

SOCIAL NETWORK PHOTOGRAPHY
Copyright © 2011
Gofresh GmbH
Lilienstr. 1
81669 München
Germany
www.gofresh.de
Kontakt: buch@gofresh.de

Alle Rechte, insbesondere das Recht der Vervielfältigung und Verbreitung, vorbehalten. Kein Teil des Werks darf in irgendeiner Form (durch Fotokopie, Mikrofilm oder ein anderes Verfahren) ohne schriftliche Genehmigung reproduziert oder unter Verwendung elektronischer Systeme vervielfältigt oder verbreitet werden.

1. Auflage 2011
www.socialnetworkphotography.com

Autoren:
Laura Piantoni
Sabine Irrgang

Art-Direktion & Design:
David SAID Mayerhofer

Alle in diesem Buch genannten bzw. abgebildeten Firmenbezeichnungen, Firmenlogos, Produktnamen, Marken und eingetragenen Warenzeichen sind Eigentum ihrer jeweiligen Inhaber.

Gedruckt in Deutschland:
WKD Offsetdruck GmbH, Ismaning

ISBN 978-3-00-033747-5